Her Turn

One Woman's Journey Through Her
First Year of Grieving

Her Turn

One Woman's Journey Through Her

First Year of Grieving

PHYLLIS DEWEY

Copyright © 2021

Phyllis Dewey

All Rights Reserved

ISBN: 978-1-7-7364347-4-1

Cover Design by Phyllis Dewey

Interior Design by Phyllis Dewey

Author's photo by Phyllis Dewey

All rights reserved. No part of this book may be reproduced in any form without written permission from the publisher – other than "fair use' as brief quotations embodied in articles and reviews.

Author Notes:

Her Turn was written in two parts.

Part one is the true personal story of the author. Any names used within the story have been changed.

Part Two is the author's insights to help others deal with the grieving process and strictly her opinions.

Table of Contents

Title	Page

PART ONE

Prologue	3
Chapter One......Rocking Chairs and Moonshine	5
Chapter Two.....Baby Steps	11
Chapter Three...A Photo is Worth a Thousand Words	19
Chapter Four.....The Waves of Grief	23
Chapter Five.....Being Positive is Okay	31
Chapter Six......The Walk Alone	39
Chapter Seven...Smiling Again	45
Chapter Eight.... Determined	53
Chapter Nine.....Life Interrupted	61
Chapter Ten......Holidays and Celebrations	69
Chapter Eleven...One Year – I Made It	81
Chapter Twelve...I Understand	89
Epilogue...........What's Next ?	93
Epilogue #2........ Year Two	95

PART TWO

Introduction	101
Chapter One....Stages and Emotions of Grief	103
Chapter Two....What to Do Following Their Death	129
Chapter Three...Becoming the New You	139
Chapter Four....Be Prepared	147
Chapter Five....Unexpected Reality	163
Chapter Six.....Living After Death	169
Conclusion	173

Part One

My Story

"*Until death do us part'*. We never think much about those words when we all say them at our weddings. They are very powerful words. Those of us who have lost a spouse continue to love even after death. Our love never dies.

There is no *'Until death do us part.'* When it comes to the emotion of love.

There is *'Forever and beyond.'*

This book, Part One, is my story. A story I never imagined I would ever write. I've been a writer since I was eleven years old when I began writing poetry. Over the years, I continued to write poetry and a couple of books that I never published. In 2019 I became serious about writing and started a book series for publication.

Then life turned on me.

This is the story of my positive journey through the first year of grief after my husband died. We had known each other for over forty years. We had spent thirty-two years together, physically and emotionally. Our love for each other kept us together even during times we were physically apart.

This is a true story. If you are living with the loss of a loved one, I hope this will inspire you to move forward and enjoy life again. While it is not easy, it is possible.

Prologue

"Goodbye" was nothing more than a way to say, "See you later." I had not even uttered that word the night I left his hospital room after his surgery. I simply said, "I love you most. See you in the morning."

And I did.

I did love him most.' It was a part of the way we always said we loved each other. We went beyond the 'I love you more' phrase. I usually won the banter back and forth of how much we loved each other. Sometimes I let him win. We would take it to 'I love you most-est-er.' And then we would chuckle because we knew there was no winner. We loved each other through thick and thin. We loved each other no matter what we were going through. If/when you ever hear our full story, you'll understand.

I did see him the next morning. It was a rough day as he was not recovering as well as I thought he should be. They still wanted to send him home – until the last minute. His vitals were not well enough to release him. I wanted to stay. He said he was in good hands and for me to go home and get some rest and take care of our dog. So, when the medical staff entered the room to take more tests, starting with an X-ray to see if pneumonia had set in his lungs, I went home. I kissed him, said I'd see him in the morning, and that I loved him more. I told the nurse I was available all night and to call me if anything happened.

I never said "Goodbye'. It was always "See you later, Babe." Even in the end, I told him, "Love you more." I never did say, "Goodbye."

That next morning, one of the many mornings in my life, is the one I will never forget. That morning changed my life like no other morning ever had. That morning I learned to listen to the medical staff. I leaned on others like never before. I began to pray longer, more often, and harder. I reached out to everyone he and I knew, our friends, friends of friends, and even strangers, and asked them to pray for him. I believe in God. I believe in miracles. I believed there was hope. I trusted God. That morning my world stopped and nothing else mattered except being with him.

That defining morning my husband coded. The nurses revived him; however, he never responded again. A lot of things happened in the next several days and weeks. Less than two weeks later, I had to make a decision no one should ever have to make. I had no real choice. Family and friends stood behind my decision. It was what the love of my life would have wanted. He never wanted to suffer. He never wanted to be in a nursing home. Especially if he was always and only going to be in a coma, a vegetable, totally reliant on others to care for his *Every* need. He would never have wanted to be hooked up to a ventilator, wires, monitors, and modern medicine, with the only purpose of keeping his organs functioning for the rest of his life. That certainly would be no way of living his life. Not for him. I knew him. His family and friends knew him. That was not for him. And so, fifteen short days after a surgery that was supposed to ease his pain and make his life better, I, along with our close family, gathered around his bed. We held his hands, brushed his brow, told him we loved him, listened to his favorite songs, watched the monitors, continued to pray, held on to him, and watched him take his last breath.

This book is the story of the immediate moments and the year that followed. The story of how I kept going became strong and stronger, and how I stayed positive and found a new me.

Chapter One

Rocking Chairs and Moonshine

The goodbyes had been said. The tears that would last longer than ever imagined had begun to flow. Mentally I knew I knew I had to take care of certain things. Physically I could not stand up. My daughters eased me into a chair and made me eat an entire snack package of peanut butter crackers to gain enough strength to stand on my own two feet. I had never felt so weak. So helpless. I pushed through. The nurse handed me papers to sign for the release of his body for his organs and tissues to be used. Family hugs were held long. I even hugged the two male nurses who were there. Those two had been the best we could have asked for during my husband's stay and for us during that time.

Reluctantly we physically left him, left the room, left the hospital, and walked away. Into a new life. A life that, at that moment, held fear, uncertainty, panic, disbelief, sadness, heartache, pain, and the strongest desire to run back inside in hopes that it had all been a bad nightmare. I stayed strong. Or maybe it was already that feeling of being numb—that feeling that would linger in the background - Grief in its rawest form.

I took a deep breath while standing in the parking lot of the hospital. I was stepping into a life never before lived by me and never planned. I looked around. To the sky. To the mountains. To my family. And one last look at the hospital. The hospital that in my mind had taken his life.

My life and the life of our family had to go on. There were family and friends to notify by phone. Additionally, over two hundred people who followed us on a Facebook group I had started needed to read the news. *"It is with a heavy heart......."* Everyone's prayers to God changed. Instead of for my husband, the prayers were for our family and me. Prayers for peace, comfort, strength. Prayers for God to put His arms around us all. Those prayers worked. The prayers before his death worked as well. God had a plan. His plan was different than what we mortals here on earth wanted. I truly believe this.

Home. My son drove me home from the hospital. We had planned it that way because as strong as I knew I was and had been the whole time my husband had been in the hospital, I knew I would not be able to drive after he died. I was so grateful for our children being there for me. And thankful his sister had come to stay with me for most of the week after he had coded. I am not sure how I would have made it through without her with me.

Yes, home. A chance to take a deep breath and to relax. My family watched as I think I walked through the house, looking at everything in a different light. A single light. I was alone. Alone in my thoughts for a few moments as I quietly talked to him, saying my goodbyes in my own way. My goodbyes that would continue for a long time; the goodbyes we never said to each other, I then silently expressed wishing he could hear me.

My family wanted to know what they could do to help. 'Hold me. Tell me it is all a nightmare!' Instead, I had them help with the phone calls and messages. And then dinner at our favorite restaurant. Yes, we went out to eat at his favorite place, some ordered his favorite meal, followed by his favorite dessert. I had my usual - lasagna. Our favorite waitress had been wonderful to us while my husband was in the hospital and continued to be amazing.

When we returned home, my son wanted to know what he could do. He needed things to keep him busy. He needed to stay busy to handle his way of grieving—no visible tears. Inside I knew he hurt. I knew it was his way. I had spent a lot of my life non-emotional. I always kept busy. I accepted life and what it handed me. My thoughts had always been: Life happens. Death happens. This time it was different for me. This time I cried. I cried hard. My son was the strong one. He was the man of the house now. Even though he was an adult and didn't live there, he would stay with me for a while and wanted something to do.

I glanced around and knew instantly—the two rocking chairs. They needed assembling. My husband had bought them with the plan to wait until we had remodeled our deck to build them. The rocking chairs were supposed to be for us to sit in, watch the mountains behind our home and grow old together. Now, I wanted them built. I would sit and rock in them as I grew old in his memory. I quickly learned not to hold things off for 'someday.' Don't keep the best for the special occasion. Every day is a special occasion. A day to cherish.

My son had the chairs built and ready to use in less than two hours. I went outside and sat for a few moments. Something was still missing in that setting—something besides my husband.

Moonshine. Yes, the real stuff. That was missing. There was still some left in a jar in the pantry. It was time to raise the first of many toasts to the love of my life, the father and stepfather to our children. I gathered everyone there around and offered each a drink to raise in a toast. Then standing on the deck overlooking his favorite view, we lifted our glasses. Once again, we sent our love, said another goodbye, and took a sip of Apple Pie Moonshine. Real moonshine made in the Mountains by a friend of my husband. Thank you, Mark. And we cried.

The next week was almost a blur, as some will understand and most would imagine. Trust those who have lost a spouse; there is no way to imagine how it feels. Everyone's story is different. Everyone has different circumstances. Everyone reacts differently. We all feel the pain. We all hurt like never before. We wish that pain on no one – ever.

A week after his death, we had a memorial 'Celebration of Life' service for him. It was different from most memorial services—those who attended commented as such. Several told me it was beautiful. I was glad. My husband had wanted a wake. He wanted a party. He had often told me that he wanted to be propped up in the corner during his wake. Sorry. That did not happen. The memorial service was as positive and uplifting as it could be. I read a five-page eulogy I had written about him and our life together. I then read a poem I had written that morning when I first woke up. My son-in-law read a two-page eulogy that he had written. We all cried. Our grandchildren cried even harder. Two ladies we had known for several years sang two of his favorite songs. A band led by our good friend played and sang three more songs.

The minister, who was a friend of ours, spoke. While there were not a lot of people there, the important people were. The people who lived out of town or out of state could not make it sent their condolences. After the service, I invited the close family to join me at our favorite restaurant. When we were seated and deciding what we wanted to eat, the restaurant staff served us a choice of my husband's or my favorite desserts, even though we had not asked for them. They didn't charge us for them. It was their way of paying tribute to my husband. I was served my husband's favorite and lovingly told that this time, I did not have a choice. That made me smile.

Family members who lived far away left later that day. Other family members left the next day.

The day after everyone who lived out of state went home, my daughter and grandson kept me company. He was taking his grandfather's death hard. I think them spending time with me was more for him than it was for me. We talked about his Papaw. He asked me what his favorite flower was, and I told him it was the Mums in fall. About a month later, he told me he wanted to make a list of all the things Papaw was missing. I asked him what he was missing. He told me the one thing was his birthday party. My grandson turned seven years old two months after losing his Papaw.

By the end of the weekend of the memorial service everyone had left. I was alone. Physically alone to figure out life. I still had the support and the connection to close family. My children and their families, his daughter and family, and his sister were phone calls and chats away. My house – was quiet.

PHYLLIS DEWEY/HER TURN

Chapter Two

Baby Steps

Waking up alone. The silence. The raging quiet pain of heartache.

Monday. Alone. I was alone in a house that no longer echoed his voice. No longer creaked from his walk down the hallway to our bedroom. A house that no longer had his breath giving it life. A house that felt empty. A house that had him everywhere, except in person. His photos were hanging on walls and resting on tables and his dresser. His paperwork was still sitting in the office: his tools, his truck, his trailers, his life. The memories of the life we had shared in this particular house for fourteen years were all here. Except he was gone.

I went numb.
I cried.
I yelled.
I hit his pillow.
I was angry.
I was grieving.
I was ---- normal.

I started researching the stages of grief. I looked for sites that talked about grieving. I looked for a list of what I needed to handle. I looked for help. I looked for articles on coping through grief through losing a spouse. I could not find what I was looking for, not specifically. So the day after his memorial service, I started writing my personal process. I didn't care how it sounded. I didn't pay attention to the spelling or if my sentence structure was correct. I simply wrote.

I introduced *After Goodbye* as a page in my writing blog, *The Flowing Pen Writing Corner*. It was my way to let others know how I was actually feeling, what I was going through, and what I was doing. The writing was my release to get through most days. My therapy. Some days were too difficult to deal with, and I could not even write. My life continued despite the roughest days. I wrote in the blog quite often at the beginning of my journey. As time went on and I felt better, felt less pain, and felt that my life was moving forward, I wrote less often on that page in my blog. Writing it helped me get through so much. When I had no one to talk to or no one I thought would understand my emotions, I wrote my thoughts and feelings. People would either get it or not. They would also see how I was able to stay positive through it all. Words. Writing. My therapy.

I spent hours wishing, wondering, thinking back to the 'what if' things. I knew I could not change a thing that had happened. Deep within myself, I understood that. I knew dwelling on it was not helping me. But I did it. I think we all do it. I am sure my family and friends even look back with what they knew about the situation and wonder 'what if.' It was too late to change even one thing, hesitate one short moment, or erase the whole nightmare. It was all done. All except the tears, the paperwork, the legal stuff, and whatever else needed completion during those first few weeks that had yet come to my mind.

I remember I cleaned the house. Every single day! Vacuumed, dusted, put everything where it belonged. The house was cleaner at that point than it had ever been when he was alive and certainly more than when we had our dog. I wanted my house to be clean in case I died, and they found me inside. I didn't want the house to be a mess. I know you are either shaking your head at me or agreeing with me. It was one of those things that, at the time, I had to do. People told me to stay busy. Cleaning kept me busy.

I also cleaned the room in my house which was a combination office and art room. The office section was the first to be cleaned up and organized. I had gone through the pile of papers and stuff he had put on the desk within ten days of his death. I was searching for important papers I needed. I was searching for photos that I could use at the memorial service. I was searching for the top of the desk that I had not seen in maybe a year. I found all I was looking for. I was thrilled to find the top of the desk. I then made it my own. I made it *my* writing desk. Over time I organized more of that room and even moved furniture around. It was part of finding and making the 'new me.'

We had the memorial service instead of a funeral and no burial since he was cremated. That was one thing he and I had talked about over the years. There was so much we had not talked about regarding what would happen when one of us would die. We avoided that topic. We knew we were getting older, and we continued to deny that death was inevitable. He told me he would die first. I brushed his thoughts aside. I advise everyone to talk about what you want to have happen when your time comes. Have things at least discussed if not fully covered, so your family does not have to figure it out at a time when they are not thinking clearly. A time when others may be pushing you to do things you do not want to do, and you are too numb at that time to say no. Voice your thoughts and opinions to your loved ones before it is too late.

Instead of a burial plot in a cemetery, we scattered his ashes. On my sixty-third birthday I went with our daughters, their spouses, and our two grandsons to the location I chose to scatter his ashes. My son could not get away from Army duties to join us because he had been away for several weeks already. I know he had us in his thoughts. The location I had chosen had been special to us since 1989 when he first brought me to Tennessee. The top of Roan Mountain, Tennessee. The sight of the old Cloudland Hotel.

In 1989 we rode his motorcycle from Pennsylvania to Tennessee to see his parents, and we took a trip to Roan Mountain. Years later, we got married at the campground below there. It became a common destination for our day trips. He loved the mountains. He told me that he would move further up into the mountains into a tiny house if I were to die first. I know that is what he would have done. And so it was fitting that his resting place is on top of the mountain.

While we were at the site I said a few words to give him a final goodbye. We played "Go Rest High on That Mountain' by Vince Gill on Spotify. I still love to listen to that song. When I hear it now, sometimes I smile, sometimes I still shed a tear. It is on my favorites list on my Spotify. We all cried. Even or maybe especially, our grandsons cried.

After we scattered his ashes, we all turned to leave. My son-in-law asked me if I was ready to leave. I said that I was and turned to join the rest of my family. Then I knew I was not ready to leave him. I was not ready to move forward. I was not ready to leave him alone there on the mountain top. I needed more time. I told my son-in-law, "no," I needed more time. He told me to take all the time I needed. I walked to the edge where the stone wall stood and said a few more goodbyes. I told my soulmate I would be okay, that we all would be okay and that we would see him again. I told him that I loved him *more*. Then I turned and went to join my family.

My grandson was having a rough time with it. My stepdaughter took time to talk with him. I am not sure what she said to him. I only noticed them as she handed him a flower, and he started to walk toward the edge where we had scattered his Papaw's ashes. His father started to chase after him, but I held out my hand and told him to let him go. He needed his own private time with Papaw. It was only a moment later, and he came running back to join us. I never asked him what he did or what he said. I hope he will always remember that special time. I hope he will always remember how close they were. He was only six and a half when he lost this important man in his life.

His family from Pennsylvania had to leave for home soon after our time on the mountaintop. It was a sad day for all of us. After six weeks of an emotional roller coaster, physical and mental pain, sorrow, mourning, grief, and leaning on each other, suddenly it was all over. The painful formalities that follow a death were over. Now, it was time for life to return to the living. For each of us to somehow continue living. To keep moving. I hoped and prayed they would be okay. I know they were heartbroken. I knew the grief would surround us for the rest of our lives. I knew we each had to move forward.

At the end of that day I knew it was time for me to take another baby step forward. I did not know what that step would be; I only knew I had to keep going. I had already taken care of so many things. Things that I had read that had taken others much longer to face. Personally, I felt the need to handle those things as soon as possible because I had no idea how I would handle them later on. I was through the mourning phase. I was now grieving, and even though I felt positive about moving forward, I knew I would have setbacks. So for me, I had to handle the important things as soon as I could. I had already taken care of the life insurance and Social Security. I had all the vehicles changed over to my name, changed the bank accounts, paid off the credit cards, and closed his bank accounts. I shut his phone down and returned it. We had purchased the phones recently and were paying for them. I deleted everything from his phone first, putting all the photos onto my computer. I took care of whatever business dealings he had. He had an Etsy shop and an eBay shop that I kept on 'vacation' while I figured out what to do with them. I later closed them both.

Within days after we scattered his ashes, it was time for me to return to work. My employer had been more than generous in giving me as much time off as I needed. I had taken two months total. The first two weeks were because I was sick and dealing with my own medical issues. The rest of the time off was associated with my husband's surgery, death, and time to grieve. I was ready. I hoped.

First, I had to handle the four-week anniversary of his death. I realized that in the beginning I counted the days, then I began to count the weeks. Then I counted the months and the weeks. At the end of this book, I guess I will start counting the years and the months. Eventually, I will count by the years. *Eventually.*

I remember watching the clock on several of the Saturdays over the months. I watched for the exact time he took his last breath. Over time I was able to get through the Saturdays without that. I have yet to get past a Saturday without thoughts of him. Without acknowledging to myself that he passed away on a Saturday. In time I was able to get to the end of the day, look at the clock and tell myself I had made it. I had made it through a Saturday. The smiles came easier over time. The Saturdays became easier.

My husband enjoyed a drink of bourbon from time to time. We had been to Kentucky to visit his cousin and enjoy some of the Bourbon Trail tours two weeks before his surgery. He had filled his own bottle of Knob Creek 125 Proof bourbon, complete with his fingerprint on the cap. When we got home and he opened it, he tossed the cap. Now, I wish I had kept it. He only had time to have a few drinks from that bottle before his surgery. I started having a drink from that bottle on Saturday nights as a toast to him in his memory. It took a while, but I did finish that bottle and the bottle of Maker's Mark that he had also started.

We were not big drinkers, but he did enjoy an occasional drink. I liked an occasional glass of wine. It wasn't until after his passing that I drank bourbon. Still not a big drinker. For several months I had a glass of wine every night and then a drink of the bourbon on Saturdays. I thought the wine helped me relax and to sleep. So did the bourbon. Gradually I broke myself of what had become a habit. I knew I didn't need it for anything. I still enjoy a glass of wine from time to time. The bourbon? I bought a new bottle of Knob Creek 100 proof. This time I am saving it for special occasions. Our anniversary, the anniversary of his death. Not every Saturday anymore.

One thing I found comforting over the first month was the sympathy cards. I used to think how lame most of the cards I saw in the store were. The words didn't seem enough to me; until I was the one who was receiving them. I took the time to read each one—more than once. I would read who sent it and feel their love. I was touched by each one. They meant a lot to me. I have kept each one. I also used to think that sending a sympathy card a week or more after someone died was horrible. To me, it felt like I had either forgotten or didn't care enough to send one immediately. I will say, those that sent them at a later time were also special. They were a help in my grieving process. They made me feel like others were still remembering. They were still grieving as well. For me, those cards that arrived later told me that others were still thinking of him and thinking of me. They were sending their love and sympathy after most had sent cards, attended his memorial, and gone on with their lives. So, for those who know of someone who recently lost a loved one, send those cards. Even if you think a week or two later may be too late. Yes, they may bring more tears, but they mean a lot. They help with the baby steps forward.

PHYLLIS DEWEY/HER TURN

Chapter Three

"A Photo is Worth a Thousand Tears"

I returned to work one month after the love of my life died. Was it a good thing to start on that date? I did it, hoping that I would not spend all day thinking about the fact that it had been one month. It worked. My co-workers were there for me and offered their condolences. I had been in to visit a few times before I returned to work, so many had already given me hugs and said their kind words.

It felt good to be back to work and to see everyone. It was also difficult. I worked retail. I had several customers who have gotten to know me over the nearly eleven years I had worked there. I had gotten to know many of them enough to consider a few to be friends as well as customers. They know a lot of my life story. Upon my return, some were learning for the first time about the death of my husband. I found my strength and was able to tell them without crying all the time. I appreciated their kind words and their hugs.

While at work, I found I missed seeing him stop in while he is out and about or in the store doing the shopping. He was the one who did most of our grocery shopping. He was the one who did ninety percent of the cooking. I was spoiled, I admit it. More difficult than going back to work was the need for me to do the shopping. I hate shopping no matter what kind of shopping it is. Now it became a part of the new me I was creating. Yes, I still hate shopping.

In the beginning, when I would come home from work or errands, I would see his photos, and I would break down. Sometimes a single tear or two. Sometimes a downright river of tears. I missed him. I still miss him. I missed what we had. I missed what we would not have together anymore. I missed his smile. I missed his quiet manner at home. I missed watching him with our German Shepherd. (I re-homed her to my daughter, son-in-law, and grandson). I missed watching him sleep. I missed his hugs. I missed his cooking. I missed our trips. I missed our day rides. I missed - everything. Looking at his photos only brought the pain of his death back along with the fountain of tears.

Then I remembered something I had been told over thirty-five years earlier. "Put the photos away. Looking at them when you can't be with them is not helping you move forward." While the advice came at a different time in my life during very different circumstances, it was still true in my current situation. So I put most of the photos of him alone and of us in a dresser drawer. Believe me, that wasn't easy to do. To close the drawer on him and hide him from me hurt like hell. From time to time, I would get them out and hold them in my hands. Sometimes only one of them, sometimes all of them at the same time. They were all I had left of seeing his face. (Although his face was/is still on Facebook).

In time I was able to get some of them back out. Now when I look at the photos, I can remember when and where they were taken and smile at the fond memories. I sometimes still shed a tear when I look at my parents' photos, who have been gone many years, so I know I will do the same with his photos. And the memories.

While I'm on the subject of his photos and them being a thousand tears, I am reminded of the weekend of my birthday, when we scattered his ashes, and his daughter and son-in-law and grandson from Pennsylvania were here. We took time to go through the boxes and totes of *stuff* in the garage and the shed. I had already gone through several of them before they arrived. I wanted her to take home the things that she wanted and that I wanted her to have that had belonged to her father. While she and I went through the boxes, we found photo albums, papers, and keepsakes that brought smiles and some tears. The photos told a lot of stories. Some we knew, some we had no idea what they were, or who they were as they were from his childhood. I gave her most of them. They were from a time before I was part of their family as her stepmother. While I did know a lot about that time in their life, I knew she would like to have them.

I have gone through most of the photos from his early life. I still have boxes full of the years we were together. When I get to them, I know there will be more tears, more smiles, a few laughs, and at least a few scrapbooks made out of them.

What did we learn in going through all of those things? While going through all the photos, Facebook posts and videos, and even the voice messages? Take the photos! Take the videos! Record the voices! Make the memories! Family time. Cherish it. Value it. One day it will be all you have left.

When all you have left are the photos, do your best to smile at the good times you had together. Laugh at crazy faces you made in photos you hated that you held on to them. Shed a tear of love. Until you can deal with the pain and sorrow they cause, put them away. Save them and let them bring you joy, smiles, and good memories when you are ready.

His daughter was one who never erased a verbal or text message. Now she was so glad. She pulled them up and saved the ones she wanted, so she has his voice. Believe me though, hearing his voice brings more tears than looking at photos. It brings a harder realization that not only is he not there to see, but he is not there at the end of the phone, or the video, or the face time anymore. There are no more conversations.

Another thing I learned while going through the photos is the need to write on the back of them or write beside them if they are in a photo album. You may know who, what, where, and when, but the other family members may not, and the next generation certainly won't. I know it is a hard habit to get into, and I am as guilty of it as anyone. I will try my best to do better.

One thing I heard about photos is to add why the photo was taken, why at the angle, and the reason. This process will put a short story about each photo and make it more special. None of us take the time to do that.

As I write this today, I have reached the nine-month mark. I am finally at the point where tears do not form rivers. They still come, and they always will, and at the least expected time.

Chapter Four

The Waves of Grief

Life started to move forward. I started to move with it. I was back to work. I was staying strong. Several people told me how amazed they were that I was so strong and handling it all so well. I thanked them and told them I was doing my best. What they didn't see were the tears at night. What they didn't see were the sleepless nights. What they didn't know was how I was still falling apart from time to time. Sometimes it was all I could do to get out of bed and go to work. Work was something I HAD to do. The rest of my day-to-day life, I often sat out. I didn't participate unless I had to. Many days, all I did was sit on the couch and watch TV, or I sat and did nothing. If you know me, doing 'nothing' is not how I am. I am a multi-tasker to the tenth power, or so some think.

I had stopped doing all my crafts. I had stopped writing my book. I had stopped reading. I could not concentrate on anything. I was lucky if I showered and got dressed. But I did. I was always afraid someone would stop by, so I made sure I was up, dressed, and my house was clean.

I used to wonder if I would become a hoarder if I ever became a widow. Quite the opposite had happened. I prefer less stuff, organized, clutter-free space.

I had been able to take care of getting the bank accounts all into my name. I was able to get all the vehicles into my name. I was able to get some of the credit cards erased because they were in his name only. (I had to close another account later because he was the primary name on it, and the account got hacked.) I was able to pay off most of the bills. I was able to get Social Security transferred from him over to me since I was over sixty years old. I was able to get done what I had to. My idea was to get as much taken care of as soon as possible, so I would not be dealing with any of it a year later. I was already determined that I was going to move forward with my life. It was something he would have wanted for me. He had even mentioned over the years that if he should die first that I would find a new man and get married again. NO. I plan to stay single. I've had the best. I am not saying 'never' because I learned a long time ago that 'never' does not work. If I say never, then chances are it will happen. I was once 'never' going to get married again. So glad I did get remarried to my soulmate. I also know that there may be another special someone out there somewhere. Time will tell.

While taking my steps forward, I bought a few things I had wanted for a while. A new camera. A new printer – only because the two we had quit. I needed a bigger one than the spare one we had that was still in a box. I use them both now. I also bought some new clothes. I cut my hair into a new style (Yes, I usually cut my own hair). I even found an amazing deal on a newer car and bought it all on my own. I did have a girlfriend go with me to make sure I asked the right questions. I also had a mechanic friend of mine check out the car before I bought it. My late husband had taught me a lot over the years. I'm so glad I paid attention. I hired a man to mow my yard and sold the two mowers I had. I was taking steps forward.

A few weeks after my husband died, I noticed the floor in my basement buckled. I was so upset over it. I called my daughter in tears. She came over, and I got my *strong* on and called the company we had used before to come set up dryers to dry out the basement. While that man was there I asked him what the issue was. He took a look around and told me that the land at the house sloped in the wrong direction. It needed to pitch away from the house. I would need dirt put in and sloped away from the house. So I made a few phone calls and two days later had dirt delivered. I made a few more Facebook contact calls, and two days after the dirt was delivered, I had four men and my grandson at my house moving the dirt for me. One man helping move the dirt looked around to see what else needed to be repaired. He spotted one thing, and two months later, he came back to fix that for me. The good news about the buckled floor was that gradually the floor went back to normal and I have not had to replace it. God is good even through the rough times.

Between the day my husband died and the memorial service, my son checked off several things that had been on my To-Do List. He replaced a toilet, installed a light fixture, and replaced the flooring on my deck. I had all the materials for all the projects. We were waiting for my husband to recover from his surgery to work on them. My son also went through the shed and organized a lot of the tools and *stuff*.

I was blessed.

With all my steps forward, you may think life for me was going a lot better than most traveling this journey. I admit I was doing well—most days. Do not let my good days fool you. I went through what most widows and widowers go through. I may have progressed quicker, taken a lot more deep breaths to get through the days, pushed harder. I was still grieving. Grieving does not end.

There are many things widows think about when this new way of life hits us. One is if or when to take off our wedding rings. Many leave them on for the rest of their lives. Others move them to the other hand. Some take them off after a while. I normally wear several rings. I always took most of them off every night except my wedding and engagement rings until March of 2019. My husband and I were enjoying, sort of, our third cruise. I interject 'sort of' because we accidentally went during Spring Break – BIG mistake. On the second day of our cruise, my hands were swelling. They swelled to the point I had to have two rings cut off. I was able to take my wedding rings off before that hand swelled too much. It was over two weeks before I was able to put my rings back on. I was only able to keep them on for a short amount of time. It turns out I am allergic to the sun and hot temperatures. It happened again while my husband was in the hospital. I was able to spend some time sitting out in the sun at the hospital while he was going through a medical procedure and when I simply needed a break. My hands started to swell again. Again the rings came off. Again I put them back on. The next time my hands started to swell, I took the wedding rings off and have kept them off. I wear my other rings again, but once my wedding rings were off that last time, I accepted that it was okay for me to take them off and store them with his wedding ring. For a while, I wore them all on a necklace. Then I even took that off. Someday I may take them all in and have a special ring or something made with them. When I'm ready and when I find something I like.

I have also learned that as many steps forward that I take, I take an occasional couple of steps back. Or so it seems. 2019 was a rough year for my extended family and me. We had lost a good friend to a heart attack in January. April 30th, my husband's cousin-in-law died of a heart attack in his sleep. My husband died thirty-one days later. His favorite Aunt died thirty-seven days later. Another cousin died in December of that year. Also that year, my kids lost a half-brother. My neighbor lost his mother. I had a few close friends pass away. And several relatives of my friends who died. It was so bad I made a list so I could keep track. All total, I had twenty deaths that I either knew the person or knew the person's relative. The sad thing is that my list for 2020 is already up to eighteen at this writing, and it is only March. (up to twenty-four by the middle of April). I was getting to the point in 2020 of breathing sighs of relief when a day would go by, and no one I knew or that was a relative of someone I knew had died.

So for each step forward I take, I am at times taken back to my fateful day when I became a widow. The tears flow again. For me and those who have recently lost a loved one, my heart aches when I hear of another person who became a widow or widower. I want to reach out and tell them it is all going to be okay. It takes time. You will have setbacks. You will cry an ocean full of tears. You will go numb. You will go through so many emotions you won't know which way is up, and you won't know if the way you feel is the way you are supposed to feel.

Many grieving people join grief counseling groups or go to individual therapy to help deal with all they are going through. I was blessed and have not attended any other groups other than the one I did attend for widows and widowers sponsored by the funeral home. I felt so out of place I was glad I had to leave after the meal to go to work. I felt awkward because I was the youngest one there. I felt out of place because, at the time, I did not know how to talk about my experience while listening to theirs. And while we ate, not many were talking even to each other. No one sat with me except the lady in charge of the group, which I appreciated. Maybe I wasn't ready for a group like that, or maybe I didn't need it.

Then, I went to the opening of a lounge in town, and the hostess introduced me to another widow. We hit it off very well while there, and even though I gave her my card to call me sometime, she never has. And that is fine. She had been a widow for over a year and told me that I was so much further along than she was at that point.

I met another widow who was looking for an all-widows group to attend. I thought about it a lot and mentioned it to my daughter. My daughter took it one step further and started a group. It is sad when your daughter knows enough widows already in her life that she can host a group at her home. The group only met once. Three of us showed up. The lady I had met who wanted the group was not one of them. It was the holidays a month later, so we canceled. A month later, the lady acting as the counselor to the group was in a relationship with a new beau and felt she should no longer be in the group. And the other lady was moving. So the group dissolved, and I have not joined any others. I believe I am doing well on my own.

I have grieving groups I belong to on Facebook. I had to limit myself on the time I spent reading two of them. I was so overwhelmed by those who were so lost and felt they could not move forward at all, even several years after their loss. I could have easily found myself drowning in that hole. I then found one for all widows who were in my age group and ready to move forward. We encourage each other and talk about our accomplishments while being there for each other when we have a down day or week. I stay on with the other groups and do my best to encourage them. I have to be careful and not get pulled down into the sadness of loss. It is so easy to fall back. I have to keep my eyes looking forward to the new me that is waiting.

Several months after my husband died, I found I was still informing people that he had passed away. Sad when I think about it. I was adjusting to my new life while reliving that day as I told people he had passed and briefly how it happened. Many of those I was still telling six months later were 'close' friends. Yet, they didn't know. I admit I had not put his obituary in the paper. I did have it written on the funeral home website, my Facebook, his Facebook. Friends and family shared the news. I had posted it on the page for prayers I had created on Facebook. Six months later, I found I was the one comforting those I had to tell. Why was I the one comforting others? I wondered that myself at first. Then I realized why. By then, I had time to process the facts. I was moving forward. When I told them, they were hearing the news for the first time, and it was a shock to them. Of course, I had to comfort them. I was telling them it was okay for them to feel their grief. I assured them I was doing fine. The truth was that even on my bad days, I would tell most people that I was doing okay or even good. And after a while, on most days, I was.

When I have my rough days, I deal with them. I give myself that time to cry, to miss him. To miss what we could have had. I permit myself to have a bad day. Then I pick myself up by the bootstraps and move forward again.

It is all a part of me being positive. It is my way of taking as many steps forward as I can.

PHYLLIS DEWEY/HER TURN

Chapter Five

Being Positive is Okay

You have permission to smile. You have permission to breathe. You have permission to laugh. You have permission to carry on and have a good time. You have permission to move forward. You have permission to have a life of your own—a life with other people.

The loss of your loved one, even your spouse, does not mean that your life also stops. You need to go on with life. I know it seems impossible. You may not want to live without them. You will feel like all you want to do is stay in bed, and all you can do is cry. The least little thing, heck, *Everything* makes you cry. Life as you knew it has forever changed. I get it. I have been, and I am there with you.

During the first few days I thought I would never smile. Not a real emotionally charged smile. Laughter was not even on my radar. I was never going to laugh again. How could I? The person who helped me smile and laugh was gone. The good times we had together were over. How was I ever going to enjoy life again? Was there life after death? My life after his death?

Then one day, I had a visitor. It was the day of his memorial service. The house was full of the family getting ready to leave to get to the church. I was sitting on the couch looking out the front window. I have no idea what my thoughts were. I do not remember anyone talking, although knowing the people there, I know they were. Then I spotted a red-bellied woodpecker sitting on the front porch railing. I only remember seeing a woodpecker one other time in the fourteen years we had lived there, and that time it was pecking at the tree in the front yard. This one sat there long enough for me to silently talk to it. All I said was, 'Well, hello there," then it was gone. I will never forget seeing it, and I did not make a big thing of it at the time. I did not even mention it to anyone when I saw it. It was my private moment.

A month or so, I heard a noise on my back deck. I had not noticed anyone pull into the driveway, so I wondered who or what was making that rapping noise. I was busy chatting with a friend of mine on Facebook at the time. I told him I would be right back. I got up and went to the back door. There was a red-bellied woodpecker. He stayed long enough for me to see him. I smiled, said, "Hello," and then he flew away. It got me thinking. Some people say that Cardinals visit them. Others have butterflies (I already had the butterflies, and those are my Mother). Now it seemed I had a red-bellied woodpecker! I needed to know what it meant to see if it had any significance or any type of message for me. I am a Google nut and will look up almost anything. If anyone ever goes into my search history, do not be concerned. Remember, I am a writer. This time I looked up the meaning and significance of a woodpecker. I had to smile when I finished reading the article. Of course, I cried first.

It was my sign. The ending of the article stated: "The woodpecker comes with the message that you have the foundation, and it is now safe to follow your own rhythm." WOW! That sent me a strong message. One that has become my motto. "Follow Your Own Rhythm." My husband had sent me a message through this beautiful creation of God. Together they were telling me I would be okay. I could move forward. I could do things in my timing, my way, and be confident about it because of all that I had experienced and already endured in my life. I could *Follow My Own Rhythm* as I went on with life.

I created a picture of a woodpecker along with that sentence that stays on my refrigerator. I made a vinyl decal for the back window of my car with that phrase. I have a personal license plate that is as close to that meaning as I could get. There are days when I get down and all I want to do is stop the world, curl up and hide. Then I see that and smile. It is my sign that I have my late husband's approval to not only move forward but also to follow my own rhythm. So I take it literally and, for the most part, have been doing things that I have wanted to do—my way.

Doing things *my way* includes changes around the house. I began making changes almost immediately. One of the first things I changed was to hang new curtains in the living room and install a new curtain rod with matching curtains in my dining room. I had wanted them for years. I had wanted one style and he wanted another style. They are now hanging nicely, in my style. As time progressed, I made new curtains for all the other rooms in the house. I painted the front door red. I repainted the spare bedroom, which is also my grandson's room when he is here. I painted the walls in my bedroom a new color; I rearranged some furniture; I moved his bed to the basement to make another spare guest room. We had adjustable twin beds that raised the head and the feet as it was the only way he could sleep. I decided that having a spare bed was great for guests as long as it was in a different room, so I had my children move the one bed downstairs one day. I refinished the coffee table. A few months later I refinished matching end tables. The neighbor volunteered to power wash my front porch in the fall of 2019, and in the spring of 2020, I stained it. I changed some of the decorations that hung on the walls.

I went through his closet and his dresser. I saved some of his clothes. I gave a few shirts to his daughter. I saved two t-shirts and had a friend make a pillow for my grandson. I gathered his shoes. I donated clothes, shoes, unopened bottles of shampoo, conditioner, deodorant, toothpaste. Anything that I would not use that someone else would be grateful to have. That day was emotional.

I had heard of a local place that was a Godsend for those in need. They accepted donations of almost anything and sold some of the clothes for fifty cents apiece. I hated giving away the shirts that he cared so much for and took good care of them to be sold cheaply. I debated over it for several days before I took them. I walked into the store area before I went to the donation door located in the back of the building. While I stood there looking around, two men were in line to buy one shirt each. The second man, the one right in front of me, had picked up a red shirt covered with Christian sayings. So far, so good. He asked the cashier how much it was. She told him it was fifty cents. He hesitated before he reached into his pocket and pulled out some change. He said, "I don't think I have enough," as he handed her what he did have. She counted it. I silently counted along with her. No, he did not have enough. She smiled, looked at him, and said, "this will be plenty." He smiled big, said "Thank you," and walked out, thrilled to have a great clean t-shirt. I knew then that this place was exactly where my husband would want his clothes to be donated.

I had a yard sale selling some of his stuff and some of mine. I planned to have another one in the spring with his tools and more of my stuff. It was not that I did not have the room for everything. Nor was it that I was downsizing and moving. It was that I do not need all the stuff. I was following my rhythm and moving forward. Why should I hang on to things I would never use when someone else can use them? Oh, do not worry, I kept the best of the toolboxes and several of the tools that I would use. From the sale money, I planned to buy a few newer tools that I would use. Of course, our children and grandchildren will have the first choice of tools before I sell them.

At a little over nine months into my journey, I was reminded that we had been on a cruise a year before. I saw the photos and shed a few tears. Then picked myself up and put myself to work. I went outside and dug up a large area of dirt that had been in a pile for the previous eight months prior. I leveled the dirt and made a flower garden area. It would take the rest of the year or longer to refine it to perfection, but I hoped to make it a nice flower garden. I later made three other garden spots. I was not about to let myself cry all day and feel sorry for myself. Instead, I needed to move forward and get things done. My way, my timing. It was a perfect day for it. Warm, cloudy, and the dirt was easy to manipulate.

I quickly learned that everyone grieves differently, at different times, in different ways. They move forward at different times. Even children. When I began making the changes to my house, I debated getting a new living room coffee table and end tables. Instead, I decided to sand down what I had and give them the 'farmhouse' look I wanted. I knew my grandson liked to help with things like that in the past, so one day when he was with me, I asked him if he wanted to help me. He looked at me real serious and shook his head slowly, and said, "No." I knew then that I would have to take things slow. He was not ready for me to make such drastic changes. As much as I was ready to move forward and make more changes to the house, he was not. He and his Papaw were close, and he was not ready to let go of what was. So I waited. Two weeks later, late in the afternoon, he came to me and said, "You know, Granny, I think we can sand that table now." I smiled. It was too late that day to do it, but we planned to work on it the following week. And he did help me sand it that next week. After that, he started asking me what I needed help doing. When I painted his room, he helped pick out the color and helped me paint it. He was not yet seven years old at the time. After that, when I did things and helped me, he would say,

"Granny and I are remodeling." He was proud to help me. And that will always make me smile.

Staying positive and letting others know that I was staying positive helped keep me going. People continued to tell me I was strong. When I was only three and four months into this new life, I had a few people tell me that I was so much further along than they had been at that stage. Some even told me I was further along than they are even though they had been a widow a lot longer.

I try. It is not always easy. For several years I have been doing a daily morning post on Facebook to say good morning to my friends, or *Peeps* as my husband used to call them. I let them know how I am. I try to lift their spirits up and encourage them. I also invite them to lift each other in prayer. Some days my post is short. Some days I write a longer greeting. From time to time, my *peeps* tell me that they look for my posts and that what I write is what they needed to hear, that my words or memes help them out in some way.

I look at my posts in different ways since becoming a widow and being on my own. My morning posts let everyone know I am up, awake, and mostly alive. It also is my way of sending out a positive note. Now, I will be honest, some days being positive is the last thing I am feeling. I would prefer to close all the curtains, stay in bed, and hide. I know people are counting on me to be there for them, so I get up. There are days when I know ahead of time what I am going to write. There are other days when I sit there with my fingers at the keys and say, 'Okay God, what do You want me to tell people today. The next thing I know, my post is done, and it gets more comments than others. It is not always me doing the writing. God is always with me.

I have a strong faith. I rely on Him to get me through each day. I always have. I was raised in church life. I was taught the Bible. There was a time that I did walk away from it all, then several years later, I returned. My late husband gave his life to Christ in 1994. I gave my life to God many years before that. At the time of his death, we had not been to church for a few years. Our faith, our beliefs, our prayers were still strong. We had, and I still have many close Christian friends. Through my faith, prayers, and the prayers of many others, I have moved forward. It is through Him that I have the strength to carry on with my life. I praise Him every day for all the blessings, for his guidance, for the doors he has opened for me, for the doors he has closed as well. I praise Him for the talents he gave me. For the words to write each time I sit with paper, pen, computer, and thought. I don't know where I would be without Him. I don't know how I could accept death if I didn't know there was more to come in a life eternal.

As many people admire my positive attitude and the ability to keep going, I hope no one thinks that because I can move forward seemingly easy, it is easy to do. I hold myself back from doing more. I find myself in mindless thoughts at times. I find sitting and listening to music for comfort helps get me through the days. I find I still put off things I want to do and need to do. I still think there is always another day or another time to do things. All the while knowing we are not promised the next breath, let alone the next day. I do my best each day to be positive, to have a smile, a laugh, a joyful memory, a feeling of knowing that my late husband wanted me to keep going and moving forward. To enjoy life and to be happy. So I hope you also know it is great to be positive and to be happy. It's okay.

PHYLLIS DEWEY/HER TURN

Chapter Six

The Walk Alone

I had lived alone before. This time is so different. I did not ask for this. It was not part of my life plan. It is assumed that one partner will live longer than the other, leaving the survivor to live alone. Few are prepared for it. The surviving spouse faces so many decisions, decisions about the rest of their lives.

Widows and widowers come at all ages and stages in their lives. Some are young and have little children to care for and raise alone. Some are older as I am. Older widows or widowers may decide to move in with their adult children. Others will choose to live alone, at least for a while. Some will remarry. I have chosen to stay in the house we shared for our last fourteen years together. I have chosen to walk this walk alone. Friends? Yes. A new relationship? No. Am I searching for another marriage? No – not unless God opens those doors.

I may be alone. I'm not lonely. I am not isolating myself from others or life. I have family near and far. I have one couple next door which has been there for me through this. I have friends. I have people who check up on me. I have friends who I go out to eat with once in a while. Friends who offer to go with me on my short trips. I am blessed that I like being on my own. I like being able to do what I want when I want. I like eating what I want or not eating if I don't want to. I like my life. Would I prefer having my spouse with me? Of course. But I don't. Fact. Life. My life. Alone. Surprisingly to some -- Happy.

He taught me a lot during the years we were together. We spent five years traveling the country with our work. We were together twenty-four/seven for those five years while we lived in a thirty-one-foot RV. Was our marriage perfect? No. I do not think any marriage is perfect. Then again, describe *perfect*. What may have worked for you may not work for another couple. What worked for us may not have worked for you. So, to ask if ours was perfect? Well, no. We had our issues. We always managed to work our way through them. Even the time he left, we divorced and married other people. Those five years certainly were not perfect. They were not even good. And God worked to bring us back to each other. We were blessed being together for the best and last fifteen years of our lives, fourteen of which we being married again to each other.

I choose to walk my new life alone. Each day I wake up and thank God for a new day. Some mornings I wake up, look around, smile, and say to God, "Well, I'm still here." Knowing God has not taken me home yet, so I must have a purpose for being here.

I stay busy. At the beginning of my widowhood, I was told, and have read when I was doing my initial research to stay busy. For a while, I thought I was staying too busy. I was always doing something. I was cleaning, sorting through things to get rid of them, moving them to a different location in the house, making changes in the house, decluttering, reorganizing. And when I was not physically doing manual work, I was writing. I was very busy. If I was awake, I was doing something.

Now, instead of staying busy because I am supposed to, I stay busy because there is a lot to do while taking care of a home and property. I have been able to return to doing what

I am passionate about, my writing. At the time of his death, I was busy writing book two in a series. For two months, I could not bring my thoughts together to write further in the book. How could I write about a family having a great time, falling in love, getting married, or whatever happy things my characters were doing when I was so miserable and grieving. So I used what I was going through. I developed my characters a little different from what my original plan was. Suddenly I was finishing book two and started book three. I was also able to write my husband's life story. And I wrote a lot of my autobiography all at the same time. I finished all three books' rough draft by the middle of November.

I wrote and finished his life story to give as gifts to the kids and grandkids for Christmas. I also had my autobiography done enough to make me happy. I am still working on that one. I've led an interesting life, and who better to tell my life story than me? I want the true story told. And if you are reading this, you know I also wrote this within the first year of his death. (Editing was done for a few months into the second year).

I am doing life my way, my timing, alone, and loving it.

Yes, it is possible to like being alone. It does help that I am an introvert. I prefer to stay home. I am not a shopper. I do not travel much, or at all on my own – yet. We were not people who socialized by going out to parties, bars, concerts, shows, or any of that. I still am a homebody. I have so much going on in my life at home that I have to plan ahead of time to do anything that is not work or home-related.

The late evenings are the hard times for me. Night falls. Darkness arrives. I close all the curtains. I enjoy the TV or the radio and often have either one on simply for the background noise. The silence, once the radio or TV is off, can be deafening. My brain turns up loud, and I think of all the things I want to do, should have done, need to do. In the first few months, the silence brought me thoughts of him not being by my side. We used to sit on either end of the couch.

He had his laptop open on his lap, and I had mine open on my lap. We could sit like that for hours. Sometimes without even saying a word. We were still together. We did not need to say anything. Once in a while, sitting on the same couch, we would send messages to each other on the computer in Facebook chat. It usually brought us laughter as we were silly but together.

After my husband's work injury, he could not sleep lying flat, so he slept in the recliner in our living room for almost two years. Then he bought the adjustable twin beds for us, and we slept in the same room again. I am so glad for that last year we slept in the same room. Going to bed and falling asleep after he died was difficult. He had slept with a C-pap machine. Now there was silence. Over time I was able to get to sleep in the silence. I still occasionally will have a sleepless night for no real reason.

I try to get enough rest. I try to eat enough. I had lost a few pounds when he was in the hospital. I was down to the weight I wanted to be. When he died, I heard a lot of, 'remember to eat,' 'take care of yourself.' So, I did. Now I have a little weight to lose – again.

Life goes on whether you live alone, have moved to a new location, moved in with your children, or anywhere. It all has challenges. Obstacles to overcome. Emotions to handle. Goals to work to achieve.

I know I will always have memories of when we were together. I will look back at the places we went and the things we did. I will always remember being awed by his memory of places we traveled while traveling in the RV with our motorcycle business. He always remembered more about our travels than I did. I wish I had written more about our life together, places we were, things we did, and the stories he told while he was here to remind me of the things I have forgotten. He used to say he could write a book. I told him he should. He said he wasn't the writer; I was. However, we never got together to write his story. Until what I wrote after he died, and I know I missed so much.

So, even if you are not a writer, you can write down the words if you can speak. Tell your stories.

PHYLLIS DEWEY/HER TURN

Chapter Seven

Smiling Again

Smiles –
They come at the least expected moments.
They stay for brief seconds.
Eventually, they last a while.
In time they will be second nature again.
Joy and happiness will return.

You may wonder how I was able to smile during my grieving journey. How did I find any joy when I had such heartache, such pain, such loneliness, such a feeling of loss? My faith kept me going. My trust in God. My belief in Him and in His way of answering prayers. Some may find it hard to understand how I kept my faith, my trust in God. Others are amazed at my strength and my attitude. I still felt the pain. I still felt the heartache. I still felt the loneliness and the feeling of being lost without him. I know I always will feel the pain and the heartache from time to time. On more than one occasion, my husband told me that if anything should happen to him, he wanted me to go on with life and living and be happy. That was not easy to do in the beginning. In time, I looked at his photo and knew he was telling me to be happy and go live life. There were times when I would do certain things and could feel how proud he was of me. That helped me smile.

There does come a time when the smiles appear easier than the tears and sadness. The heartache is not as pronounced nor constant. The physical pain of loss gets interrupted by a smile that arrives from either a good memory or from something new that makes you forget the pain and heartache, even for a brief second.

When I realized I had smiled the first time, I was shocked. I was hurting so bad. The house was full of people, and yet I felt so alone. The pain was overwhelming. For all my strength, I was not sure how I was going to make it through the days, weeks, months. Let alone the years! I did know I had to be strong for my family and ultimately for myself.

Soon after his death, my children, stepchildren, and grandsons were sitting in the living room. The left side of the couch where my husband always sat was left empty. Everyone knew that was 'his' spot. No one wanted to sit there. I didn't think anyone ever would, and I was not sure how I would react if someone did sit there. That first day I thought I never wanted anyone to occupy that special space. It would mean that he was truly gone. No one sat there even when he was away for the day at work. He was always coming home, so they left it vacant.

Until ----

My youngest grandson had other thoughts about that spot which surprised me. He was at the house soon after his Papaw had died. It could have been later that day or the next day; I don't remember. He simply walked up to the place Papaw always sat. He jumped up, turned around, and plopped himself down in his spot. "Well, I guess this is my spot now," he announced. We all looked at each other in a bit of shock. I looked at him and smiled. "I guess it is," I said as I took a deep breath and smiled.

Yes, the smiles come again. At first, when you least expect them. Then it is the little things that bring them and brighten the day.

Some of mine:

A blue bird outside my window. The cardinals in the tree out front that fly down to my porch seemingly look at me through the window. Even the robins arrive earlier than normal in the late winter. The winter that brought so little snow, I never worried about being able to get to work. The people who reached out through cards, calls, and Facebook to say hello or stay a while and chat. Little could they have known I was having a rough day when they popped up and said, "How are you?"

A room in my house that I have cleaned out and made less cluttered.

The box that was finally empty because I either put stuff away or tossed out what I didn't need.

The bills that show up with a zero balance because I was able to pay the accounts off.

Sunshine after a cloudy day.

A baby I had prayed for even though I did not know him coming home after a year fighting for his life.

My favorite photo of my grandson, that sits at the desk where I write my books.

The words of encouragement that I have placed around my house to help me make it through the rough days that tell me I am amazing or that I can do 'it," whatever "It' happens to be that day.

A tiny piece of paper of a message my son sent me that says. "I love you, too. Stay Positive,".

Friends that ask how my writing is going. Or ask how I am doing and smile when I tell them I am fine because they know I am telling the truth. At that particular moment... I am fine. They may not know that later on, I may not be. Or that earlier, I had wiped my tears dry. Most days were good – in time.

Accomplishing something easily that I thought I would have to fight for.

Able to watch a comedy on TV and laugh instead of cry.

Able to watch a show I used to watch with my late husband without turning it off because I can't stand to watch it without him. Yes, I turned some off because they were 'his' shows we used to watch together.

Shows that I now watch where before I would not have watched because he didn't like them or the actors in them.

Able to sing to music on the radio, in my car, at home, on Spotify. I never sang when we were together... I can't sing, not well, and only with the radio loud enough that no one can hear me.

Knowing who to contact when something needs fixing or when I need a professional opinion. Such as when my roof lost a shingle, or the moisture I talked about earlier, or buying my car. He taught me a lot, and I am so glad I listened. I smile because I know he would be proud of me, including replacing insulation by myself in the garage that had fallen.

Seeing a car go past me with a dog hanging out the window that looked like he was smiling. It was raining out, and he was having a great time feeling the wind and rain hit his face.

Needing a pile of dirt spread in my yard so I could plant a garden and doing it all on my own.

Yes, Smiles come when I need them and come from the smallest and the biggest of things. I am finding the smiles slowly taking up more of my time. There are so many things in life to smile about. So many things to bring joy into our lives. You can find things to smile about as well. Keep moving forward. Pay attention to the unexpected smiles. There will be more.

Again, how did I do it? I started by taking one day at a time. Some days, if I managed to breathe all day, I felt I had accomplished something. There were finally days I could get through with only a few tears and then a whole day without a tear. Accomplishments that made me smile at the end of the day. Then there were days something brought on the tears, and I let them come for only a few moments. Then I dried my eyes and got busy doing something that brought me joy and a sense of accomplishment, and the overall day was a positive one. Reaching a goal that I set for myself brought smiles.

Laughter – that is another story. Laughing is still hard. I was not a person who laughed a lot to begin with. I don't do practical jokes. Watching AFV where people fall and most people laugh, I don't. I feel their pain and possible injury. So laughter to me even before he died was difficult. Over time I found I could laugh some. Not the laughter that comes from deep inside; still, it is laughter.

The laughter and smiles come from the calves playing in the pasture behind my house, the times when I do stupid stuff, and at some TV shows. I found I could laugh out loud more. I found I could laugh at more silly things.

I realized a long time ago that life is short. Losing my soulmate so young reminded me life could end at any moment. I need to smile and laugh to keep myself feeling upbeat and positive. I want to encourage others by what I am doing and how I am doing. So I do my best to see the positive side of things. I avoid things that I cannot do anything about. I do my best not to stress over as many things as I used to. I also have an illness aggravated by stress, so it is best to avoid it.

In my first year as a widow, I found that when I started to feel down, then looked for something to lift me up; it made the whole day better. The things that lifted me up included going for a walk, watching the cows or the birds, listening to good music, working in my garden, or enjoying a piece of dark chocolate. In the years to come, I hope to continue to find things to lift me up out of my dark moments. The things that lift me may change over time, and you will find the things that lift you. Look for what helps you.

I found that the music and songs that once made me cry right after his death now usually bring a smile. The songs that were played at his memorial service that brought tears for a while gradually brought smiles, and I now play them on purpose to bring a smile and remind me of him and our love. His favorite songs eventually brought smiles as I remembered the fact that it didn't seem to matter what song was playing; if it was an oldie country song or old rock and roll, he knew the words to it. Some of his favorite songs have been added to my favorites list.

I also have found some new favorite songs of my own that make me think of him. At first, they would make me cry or at the least tear up. Now I can smile and enjoy them.

Some of his favorites include Nights in White Satin, Turn the Page, Sound of Silence, Hallelujah, A Deer Panteth, to list a few. He liked the old country artists and old rock and roll. The 1950s–1960s.

The favorites that I play to remember him in addition to his favorites include: Go Rest High on the Mountain, When I'm Gone, Sound of Silence, and I Can Only Imagine.

We had tickets to a Pentatonix concert scheduled two weeks after his surgery. It was his belated birthday present from me. I had to cancel them. I still would like to go hear them in his memory. Maybe someday if they play close to town again.

Smiles – they came more often over time. In the beginning, I thought it was bad that I was able to smile and be happy. What would people think of me if they saw me being happy when he had died so recently? It is wonderful to smile again. It lets others know it is okay for them to smile too. They didn't have to be somber and feel bad around me. They didn't have to be careful of what they said or did around me. I realized people followed my lead when they saw me smile and be positive, and move forward. When they realized I was okay with doing things the same way we had done things when he was alive, it was a relief to them. I was permitting them to live a normal life. When they could see I was okay (most days), they knew they could be okay. Some days I think I am doing better than other family and friends who still grieve for him. Everyone grieves differently.

There are so many things that can bring a smile, even if it is for a brief moment. When I wake up each morning, I first look around and realize I am still here. Here inside my room, my house, and here on earth. God has given me at least one more moment to be here and live my life. He is not ready to take me home.

Most people don't know how to behave around a person who has lost a loved one. They don't know what to say. They don't know if it is okay to have a good time, smile, or laugh around you. They don't want to say the wrong thing, so many don't say anything. They keep their distance. If you can find it in yourself to smile, be happy, and even laugh, it will let those that love you know you are okay. Your demeanor will let them know that it is okay to go on with life. Acting normal, or as normal as you can be, will help you to move forward.

I hope you can find the things, the moments, the memories that bring you more smiles than tears. Yes, the tears will always be there from time to time. It is the smiles that can become more powerful for you in your moving forward.

PHYLLIS DEWEY/HER TURN

Chapter Eight

Determined

I mentioned earlier that God wakes me up each morning because he is not ready to take me Home. He was, however, ready to take my husband. While many may question why God took their spouse, I look to God and thank Him. Yes, that is possible to do. My husband had a rough and painful life. He was told as a kid he would not live to be eighteen. Then he survived the Air Force, including time in Vietnam in the early 1970s. Later he was told he would not live to see thirty. He almost didn't. He was in a motorcycle accident and almost died in 1976 when he was twenty-one. His parents were told to call the priest and call the family. The doctors did not expect him to live. Then the doctors said he would never walk again. Then they said he would never walk with his one foot pointed straight forward. God had other plans. He gave him another chance. Less than a month after the accident, he walked out of the hospital using crutches. He was given another chance to live his life. It was one filled with physical pain every day, but it was a life to live. A life that, because of that accident and the circumstances that followed, led him to me and the life we had together.

I smile when I think of the years we had together. Those years were not easy. His physical pain, the hardships we went through over the years often strained us. In the end, when it counted the most, we were together. Those that knew us knew we belonged together. They believed we were perfect for each other. Okay, some questioned it until they understood us and admired the love we had for each other.

Our faith, my faith, is what helped us get through all the rough patches we went through in our relationship. We survived all the things that life put us through over the years. I know God has gotten me through everything so far in my life. Because of that, I can move forward. Yes, there is light at the end of the tunnel. There is light outside my door. When it gets dark outside, there is even light in my room and the house. There is a positive vibe in my life that keeps me going. There is light in my heart.

I am determined. What gives me the determination to face the next challenge? To reach for the next goal? To fight for what I want my life to be? Knowing that it can be done. I know each day will not be all sunshine and roses. Not every day will I be able to wake up, look around and breathe in the joy of having another day in front of me. I will have days when I have to do things I do not want to do. I will have days when staying in bed is still the only thing I desire. And yet, it is something I have not done during this first year. I will have days when shutting the world out is the only goal of the day. I will still get up. I will press forward. Determined. Hopeful. Deep breath. One step at a time.

Most days, I wake up ready to face the world. I have a list of things to do either in my head, written on a piece of paper, or the calendar. I know what needs to be done, yet I do my best always to give myself free time. Time to do anything or nothing. Time to sit back and relax and breathe. Time to stare out the window and soak in God's beauty that surrounds my property.

Each day, no matter how I feel, begins with prayer. It may be a long prayer. It may be a simple prayer of, "Thank you, Lord. I'm still here." Most nights, I write a prayer as part of my journal entry. My days begin with coffee. Yes, I'm a coffee drinker. Black, thank you. My mornings continue with my time on Facebook posting, so everyone knows I am still alive. I also post words of encouragement to everyone on my friends' list. Their friends can read it too. I do not make most of my posts public. Maybe I should. Except there are a few people that I do not want to know what I am doing every day. My evenings either come to a close with a glass of wine or hot tea. My nights conclude with a final look through Facebook, writing in my journal, and doing my best to fall asleep before it is time to get up again.

My Facebook presence began in 2009. I was apprehensive about joining even though 'everyone was doing it,' so my husband and I joined the masses. My morning posts became twofold after becoming a widow. I used to post to help lift everyone's spirits, encourage them, let them know I was praying for them, and suggesting they encourage others and stay in prayer. After being a widow for a few months, it dawned on me that my posts were also letting people know I was up, alive, and doing.... well, however I was doing that day. Many react, some comment. From time to time, someone will tell me they appreciate what I wrote or that my words made their day. Some have told me they look for my daily posts. I look forward to those who acknowledge my posts, as that is what helps me smile.

Life does go on. I quickly learned that I had to go on with it. If I simply sit and watch each day go by watching the sunrise out my back door and set out my front door, I will have wasted the day God gave me. Especially if I do not even appreciate that day for the gift that it is. Each day is a day to cherish. A day to be there for someone else if they need me. A day that maybe someone reaches out to me to lift my spirits and bring me a great smile.

Each day I look around me and pay attention to all that I can. I want to experience all the life God gives me. I did the best I thought I could before. Now life seems more important. So many of us go through life only doing what we have to do. We get up, go to work, go home, get some sleep, get up and do it all over again. I have learned we need to live life. Get up, do something. If it is a workday, then give that day the best you can. I try to share my smile to encourage others because I never know what they may be going through.

The customers I see at my job do not know what is going on in my life. The regulars that I have gotten close to over the years know or found out after I returned. They see my smile. They do not notice the pain in my heart. They do not see the heartache I feel some days. They do not know the feelings I have seeing married people together. When I see the older couples who are blessed to have those years together and are still there to cherish each other, they do not know that I wonder if they cherish their spouse.

I see parents with their children and wonder how much the parents love their children and give them all they can—teaching them how to treat other people—teaching them to be kind, to share, to cherish others.

I see teenagers and know they are taking life for granted for the most part. I was a teen once. Life goes on forever when you are a teen. People spend their teenage years wishing they were older so they could do more. They want to drive; they want to be out of school; they want to be out of the house and on their own. Some have dealt with loss, and they understand that life is not all a bowl of cherries. Some have lost a grandparent, some even a parent. Some have lost a friend, and some may have lost a sibling already. Again, I do not know what those carefree teens have experienced. I hope they have not yet known the pain of loss. I hope everyone appreciates life and those that are in it with them.

I want to tell people that life is short. That the fight they had in the morning, the anger they felt, is temporary. I want to tell them to take a deep breath and love each other. I know they will not listen. If I tell them that I recently lost my soulmate, they will say they are so sorry, and I appreciate that. Unless they have experienced the loss of their spouse, they do not feel what I feel. They do not understand what I am going through. They do not realize that my being there, able to tell them, may have taken all the strength I had that day. They do not realize that some days it took all I had to climb out of bed. Unless they have been there, they don't know. I realize that. I used to be in their shoes. I felt horrible when someone lost a spouse. I couldn't imagine. I was right; I could not have imagined-- until it was me. Then I learned how to move forward with life. Not like his death never happened, but like God and my soulmate would want me to continue living.

Moving forward. When we move forward, we take steps to propel us to go on ahead. We go on with our lives without forgetting those we lost. As widows (and widowers), we take all our memories of our loved ones with us as we continue living.

I moved forward a lot in my first year. Mentally I was able to change my thought process to be about me instead of us. I had over thirty years of my life being 'our' life. When he died, my life was now 'my' life. Now there is only me. It is a process to be able to think on a personal level and to think single again. I still find myself saying or writing 'we' instead of 'I,' "our' instead of 'my,' 'us' instead of 'me.' My mind knows the difference; it is my heart that does not always let go.

Moving onward. When we move onward, we do so by leaving something or some things behind. We move beyond what was. We do our best to forget the past. I know I will never forget my past with my love. I will always carry those memories. I also know that during my first year, I had been able to leave some things sitting by the roadside to be destroyed, in a manner of speaking. Things I chose not to take with me. Physically and mentally. Forgetting some things on purpose is harder than getting rid of the physical things. By moving onward, a person allows themselves to start fresh without constant reminders. Yes, I did it. I moved onward to a certain degree. How? I was able to donate his clothes and other belongings. I was able to pack up things to sell in a yard sale. I was able to sell some of the things he owned. I was able to redo part of our landscaping to be mine and not how he had used it. I was able to redo rooms in my house. Yes, I was able to think of the house as *my* house instead of *our* house. I was able to say goodbye, farewell, and even good riddance to things. A bit harsh? Not really. When you have time to think about it and are ready to move forward and move on, you will see that you like things different from what you had. You will find the new you.

You may think some of my goals to get through this were a bit odd. I may have been further along my path than you are ready to be in this first year. And that is okay. One goal I finally set for myself was to sell the flatbed trailers. I was determined that on his birthday, I was going to finally put his one flatbed trailer out there to the public for sale. I had one sitting at the house. The other was at a neighbor's barn, and when it rained a lot, it was hard to get to. So I only posted the one at the house for sale. I was unsuccessful at selling it by word of mouth to maybe go to someone I knew. So on the evening of what would have been my husband's 65th birthday, I posted the trailer online on Marketplace. And I waited. I had over 300 people look at the post. A few men sent me messages with questions about it. After a week, I was starting to think it would not sell. I had the feeling that, like so many things I had tried to sell in the past, it was going to be added to my list of failures, and I would be stuck with it until I had no other option except to give it away.

Then the nine-month anniversary of his death came and passed by. I felt different. I am not sure what changed. Nothing specific that I could put the finger on. I knew something was working in my mind to move me forward. A week later, I got a message asking if the trailer was still available. I said it was and waited for him to ask more questions about it. Instead, he only asked if he could come by later that day to look at it.

YES! It was my first real potential buyer. He sent me a message that he could not make it that first day and asked if he could come to look at it the next day. The next day he arrived when he said he would. He checked it all over. He offered me less than I was asking, adding that he would need to buy new tires for it as well as a spare. I considered that and the fact that 1) I wanted it gone and 2) he knew what he was talking about. He was a young father working a regular job, and he needed this for his self-employment job. He needed it to haul a car that weekend. I had a good vibe about him, so we compromised and agreed on the price. He paid me half down and said he would be back to get it around dinner time. Again he sent me a message that he would be late. I appreciated his communication with me. He then arrived with his stepson, who was eleven, and together they hooked up the trailer. I was impressed that he knew how to hook it all up safely and was pleased with who God had sent to buy it from me. My late husband took care of it the best he could while he used it and overused it. He was always conscious of safety. He would have approved of its new owner.

That same week the gentleman who had agreed to buy my longarm from me contacted me that he and his wife could come to pick it up. I was thrilled! The bad part is that they would not be paying me at the same time. Instead, they would pay me as they sold it. I agreed to their terms because I wanted it out of my studio to move forward with my life. They arrived on time. We had a good talk while they were there. He and my husband had been great friends and so much alike from the day they first met. I know he missed him being there. He asked how I was doing and was glad to know that I was doing fine. I think I was doing better than he thought I would be.

It was also at this time that I made my flower bed I talked about earlier. I was determined —with goals and a time frame. I was almost there —I was doing well.

Chapter Nine

Life Interrupted

Life was going well. I was adjusting to the new me. I was no longer sad or feeling so lonely in the evenings or even during the days as I had been. I was getting a routine to my life. I was finding joy in completing things I had listed to do. I was proud of myself. I had plans. I had places to go, things to do. I was finding happiness. I was making large strides in my forward movements. I was going to be fine.

THEN – the Coronavirus hit China, Europe, and then America.

Everything changed. Nothing was normal – for anyone – anywhere.

I was still working when it broke out, and I immediately did not want to be at work. I was afraid of being exposed to it, becoming sick, in the hospital, or even worse. My family had already been through enough in the last year. They had lost enough family members and did not need to lose another one. They did not need me even getting sick. I was worried. I was healthy; however, this virus was attacking the healthy, the at-risk, the young, the old; it did not matter who or what people were, they could get sick.

Then I was blessed. The company I worked for allowed all of its employees to take a leave of absence if they had the virus, felt sick, or did not feel comfortable being at work. I chatted with a co-worker who was taking advantage of the leave of absence and followed her advice. I put in for two weeks off and told them I would decide at the end of those two weeks if I would be taking more time off. Since I only worked two days a week anyway, I took eighteen days off and only missed four days of work. As the pandemic continued to infect more people and more people were dying, I took more time off work until it reached a total of six weeks that I had taken off. I only missed twelve working days while I stayed home for forty-eight days.

I did my last grocery shopping on my way home the last night I worked. I had a good supply of food that would last me for a while. I filled my gas tank, although I did not plan on going anywhere. I wanted a full tank if an emergency arose.

People in the United States were suddenly hoarding toilet paper, paper towels, hand sanitizer, bleach, and other cleaning supplies. Face masks, latex gloves, and then even foods were disappearing from the shelves everywhere. People were in a panic. They didn't know what to do. They didn't want to be stuck, alone, hungry – with no toilet paper. No one understood the toilet paper hoarding, yet so many people joined in buying as much as they could that the shelves were empty.

I was not one of the hoarders. Many years before, my husband and I started doing what we called a 'major shop' in December. The company I worked for gave the employees an extra discount to use only one day, one-time use if they worked Black Friday. I always worked that day. My husband and I took that extra discount to stock up on non-perishables that would last us a year, if not more. After his death in June of 2019, I did that same shop with my daughter's help that year. I had plenty of toilet paper, cleaning products, most food, and I was not going to panic. I would survive – alone.

During the first week of having to stay at home, I realized being alone did not bother me. If I had not been at work, I had been home most of the time anyway over the previous nine months. I was used to being 'stuck' at home. I had, however, reached the point in my new life that I was ready to go on day trips and eat out alone. I had not gone on a day trip alone. I had not braved eating out alone. And this interruption set me back a while in my moving forward process.

It also put a damper on my other plans for the next few months. I was planning a trip to Pennsylvania to visit family and friends and meet my new great-niece. I had a yard sale planned, home projects to get done. I was planning to be busy moving forward. I was hoping that in getting those things done, I would have some closure on my old life and have my new life by the time I reached my first anniversary of being a widow. So much for my plans. God had other plans.

Instead of that closure, I was now faced with more time writing this book and editing my book series. It also gave me more time for some home projects, although the rain and cooler weather hindered some of those.

Once again, life had thrown me a curveball. Becoming a widow was a hard curveball. I had been making great strides to run the bases forward to a new life with the new me. Now I was being stopped in my tracks, and someone was calling a foul.

So deep breath in. Slow breath out. Time to stay positive. Time to get busy. I was writing, reading, cleaning, sorting through more things, looking around, and seeing what I wanted to change—and looking at his photos and talking to him.

I could have spent my time wishing he was here with me. Wishing he would take all my concerns and handle them. Wishing he would be here to tell me not to worry. I could have spent my time feeling bad for myself being alone. I could have spent my time hiding in my house or stuck in my bed in tears. I could have taken several steps backward and gotten stuck in my grieving. I could have spent all my time going through the 'what ifs' again. I could have taken this as a sign that I was not supposed to move forward. Instead, I put on a smile, took the twenty-four hours God gave me each day, and I did my best to encourage others to get through this crisis. I did not fall back down. I did not have to pick myself back up and dust myself off. I was able to stay standing tall.

I did some slumping from time to time, but I was able to survive and excelled. My faith and trust in God kept me going. He had gotten me through so many other things in my life until this point; I knew He was going to keep taking care of me. If no one else was able to be there for me, I knew He would be. He would give me the words I needed to write. He would give me the things to observe outside my window and know He was there with me. He would send me the people to chat with and think about that would pull me through. As time went on, He even reconnected me to some old friends I had lost touch with over the years. While the world slowed down to almost a stop, this break in life was a blessing in disguise.

One thing that hit me about a week into my staying home during this crisis was that now there were many more people dealing with grief. True, most were not dealing with the loss of their spouse or a life partner. It was still grieving. They were dealing with the stages of grief even if they didn't know there was a label for what they were feeling. Some had lost a loved one due to this virus. Some had lost their job either temporarily or permanently. Many had lost their freedom to travel to other countries, within their own country, state, or even city. Some had lost their favorite place to eat. Some had lost their feeling of security. Some had lost their faith in humankind. Most had lost their routine. Some had lost their joy of being with other people. They lost the reassurance of a hug from a loved one or a friend. So many were feeling lost, alone, and frightened about the future. Some didn't know what the next day would bring. Some were angry. Some were in denial. Everyone seemed worried, stressed, overwhelmed, even scared.

When this crisis is over, and hopefully life goes back to normal, most will be able to get over their grief. They will forget. They may even laugh about it when they say, "Remember when...?" It will become a story they pass on to their children and their grandchildren. For us who have lost our soulmate, our grief will always be with us.

I also grieved during this crisis about what had been forced to change in my life. I grieved as I stayed home, stayed safe in self-isolation to avoid getting sick. I missed being able to go places. I missed going to work. I grieved that as my life was getting back on track and headed for a new direction, I was suddenly forced to stop and wait.

Another step backward. I am not sure if it was the combination of being in the middle of the crisis or the fact of the request, but I had an emotional setback for a little over a week. My stepdaughter sent me a message a week before Easter asking me if I had my husband's medical chart. She wanted to know if I had his heart rhythm as she wanted to have it tattooed on her arm. I said I had his medical records, although I was not ready to look at them. They were on a CD. His records were almost 3,000 pages! Yes, three thousand pages. They dated back to 2016 when he was injured. She understood why I had not read them yet. I told her I might at least skim through them to see if there was a page with a picture of his heart rhythm.

Then I made the mistake of thinking I was brave and able to handle looking at them. I was not. I did fine as I skimmed through the records for the most part. Most of it did not make any sense to me as I am not in the medical field and do not know the medical language. Then I found the pages with the nurses' reports for his last surgery up to his death. I lost it and cried most of the day off and on. Somehow I managed to sleep well that night. The next day I was still not myself. Making it worse on myself was the fact that it was Easter weekend. Why I thought it had been a good time to read them, I do not know.

So, as much as I handled my first year of grief positively, there were times when I let the tears fall and fall big time. I also knew that it was okay to have bad moments and bad days full of tears. It was okay to have those moments, those days to feel the loss, feel the pain, the heartache. To relive the moments.

I was doing better by the end of Easter Sunday. I felt proud of myself for being able to even look at the records. I even felt proud of the tears, the pain, the sadness. I was allowed to feel those feelings.

A week later, I took more steps forward and did more rearranging in my home to make it, even more, my home. Another week later, I made more changes in my house in my writing room to make it a nicer writing area.

In your time of grieving, there will be things that you won't be able to do. My kids and stepkids and grandchildren cannot read the book I wrote of his life. Not all of it anyway. I had not been able to look at the medical records. I still have not looked at them closely other than those nurses' reports. The comments in the reports that gave me smiles were when the nurses wrote, "His wife was by his side," "His family was by his side." I was in his room and by his side as much as I could. He may not have known that his family and I were there with him. We will never know.

By then, I was ten and a half months into being a widow. I was sitting back, thinking about my life and what I wanted the new me to be. It hit me. Hard. It made me smile. A lot. I. Me. The new me. I was a writer! Although I had been writing seriously since January 2019, I had not given myself the acknowledgment that that was who/what I was. Until then.

Once I could smile at the reality of taking yet another step, and it was a big step, I knew I could keep moving forward. God was with me. He would be with me no matter what I had to face.

He will be there for you. I pray you do not have to simultaneously go through this virus crisis and grief, although I know many of you did. You can look back and know you made it. Some of you may have cried yourself to sleep each night. You may have stressed. You may have lost your job; you may have suffered a great financial loss; you may have felt you could not fall any further down in your life. If you are reading this as a widow, you made it to this point. And you will make it.

Chapter Ten

Holidays and Celebrations

Following my husband's death, I did some research on grieving. I read a lot about how the holidays were the hardest time for people to get through, especially that first year. I had prepared for days, even weeks, that I would be filled with tears during the holidays. I was preparing myself for those holidays, expecting to be unable to function. I suspected there would be times I would think of him on those special days and barely be able to see through my tears. Anticipation. Prepared for the worst. Prepared to lose the strength I had gained. I was also determined to get through them. I was determined to stay strong and prove a person could get through them. I also accepted that whatever I felt and how I reacted was okay, and most everyone would understand.

And I did it. I made it through. I made it through very well—most of the time.

The first special occasion after his death was Father's Day of all days. He had been gone only fifteen days. Our tradition had simply been to go out to eat with the family that lived nearby. Usually, it was for breakfast or brunch. His daughter would also always call him. This year I joined my local family and went out for brunch. They had chosen a place my late husband and I had never been before. For me, that felt wrong. It may have been an attempt to keep me from being so sad and missing him. For some reason, all it did was make me miss him more. In addition to missing this special day, he had missed out on this new experience. In his honor, I ordered food that he would have eaten. I appreciated what they tried to do for me. I guess I was not quite ready for something new. After I got home I spent part of the day silently talking to him. Then I took a deep breath and knew, even then, that I had to be able to move forward. I knew I had major hurdles to get over for the next year. If all the articles and stories I read were true, it would be a very difficult year. I had survived the first holiday in sadness but without tears.

The next celebration was my birthday. We had never made a big deal out of it. I never had a big party with lots of people or gifts. It was always a simple dinner at the house with a cake that my son-in-law made every year. This first year without him was a little different. I had chosen my birthday to be the day I wanted the family to go with me to the mountain to spread my soulmate's ashes. You may be wondering how in the world I was able to do that on my birthday? Or why? Since from now on, not only would I celebrate my birthday, but I would also be thinking of it as the anniversary of saying my final goodbye. Honestly, I am not sure why I chose it. Maybe it was because I did not want to have another anniversary date to remember. Or maybe it was my way of him celebrating my birthday with me. My gift to him was his freedom to finally be in the mountains where he always wanted to be. Maybe it was my way of having more people here for my birthday. I look back at it now and wonder how I will feel in the coming years. Simultaneously, considering it was one of our favorite spots to visit, it was a perfect choice.

We celebrated my birthday the day before we went to the mountain because my bonus family from Pennsylvania had to leave right after our time on the mountain. They took a photo of me with my cake. I was smiling. I was hiding the pain. I'm sure if you see the photo and look into my eyes, you can see the pain. I smiled, and I enjoyed the cake. We even laughed that day. Of course, we also cried the next day on the mountaintop.

Fourth of July, Labor Day, Halloween, with other family birthdays in between, all came and went. He was missed in all of them. Fourth of July, I joined my daughter, son-in-law, and grandson to watch the parade downtown, even though that was something I had always gone to alone before. I then spent most of the day with the kids. It was a nice time, and I had fun. Halloween was one holiday we never celebrated. I always decorated the house for the fall season, and that was as far as it went. As normal, I decorated the house and enjoyed the fall season. These holidays were easy for me to get through.

We celebrated my grandson's birthday at their house, where he had a party with classmates. I don't know if he missed his Papaw on that day or not. I know he missed him in general. I missed him being there with me.

My stepdaughter had a rough time on her birthday because her dad always called her to wish her a happy birthday. He also always sent her card late. I broke that habit and did my best to send the cards on time.

Then came the BIG holidays. The family ones. The ones we had always celebrated. Thanksgiving and Christmas. The ones that some widows and widowers avoid after the loss of a spouse or even the loss of another special family member. The holidays that so many who grieve dread facing. These are never the same when missing someone who was always there. So how did I do it? Again I prepared myself. I planned early in the year. Especially this year.

As you may have figured out by now, I am a bit different. I look at life differently. I may seem a bit odd to some people. You may not understand how I was able to do what I did for those first holidays. Most people say I am strong, brave, even amazing. Some may think I am cold in my emotions. I try not to give that impression. Sometimes strength comes off as not feeling. Believe me, I feel. I have emotions. I also look at life as real. Things happen. Life goes on. Although his death hit me harder than I ever imagined it would. It was harsh. It was rough. I stood up tall against the flood of tears and sadness. I focused on the positive and the happy memories. Memories of the years we had together, the holidays we shared. I focused on the memories of the holidays I had when I was a child and the other years I was not with him. I knew putting them all together would help get me through, and I would honor them all.

By August, I had my plans set for the holidays. I had a major task I was going to tackle for the entire month of November. So I had to plan well in advance. Christmas gifts were ordered or figured out already in August or September. I usually do an ornament for each of our children and grandchildren. Those I had purchased the Christmas season the year before! I learned that trick from my Granny, who shopped for Christmas all year long. Thank you, Granny.

My task for November was to write book #3 of my series and make it at least 50,000 words. The last time I had done that challenge, it took me all month to reach that goal. In this attempt, I wanted to reach that many words, if not more, and to have time to do it, I had to have the house decorated for Christmas before November or within the first few days of the month. Yes, I had decided early on that I was going to decorate my house. I was going to decorate a lot!

Christmas had always been more my holiday than it was my late husband's. Christmas was never the same for him after age ten when his favorite Grandfather died on Christmas eve. From that time on, he was not big on Christmas celebrations. He did his best to enjoy it for the kids. I was the one who did all the decorating, bought, or made most of the gifts, and sent out all the cards. It was a tradition I kept since childhood, and he had no trouble following. When I was little, my father set up the tree, put the lights on, and sat back while watching my mother and I do all the decorating. My husband played the part my father had. He would help set up the tree and put the lights on or make sure the ones attached to the tree worked. Then he would sit back while I did all the decorating. He either watched or was not even home when I decorated the house. For the last several years before he died, our Christmas day tradition was to have brunch with our children who lived near us. After our grandson was born, we would open some gifts at their home and then have them come over to our house so our grandson could open his at our house. Since the gifts we bought for him stayed at our house to have toys here to play with, we liked him to open them here.

In 2018 we had a larger than normal Christmas celebration. My son and husband had planned a surprise for me. My son and granddaughter from Pennsylvania came as a surprise to me and spent several days. That was a great Christmas, even though my back went out and I could not walk very well for a few days. We spent some great family time together playing games, laughing, and good conversations. We drove on the racetrack in Bristol, Tennessee enjoying the lights. Then we spent time on the infield with the kids going on rides, having coffee or hot chocolate. I did some shopping. It was cold, but we bundled up, staying warm. We made memories. We had no idea what the next year would bring. I am so glad we all had that time. I am forever grateful.

In 2019 I knew no one was going to be here to surprise me at Christmas time. I had asked. Everyone would have understood if I didn't put up a tree or any decorations. They would have understood if I had closed all the curtains and doors and hid from the world outside. Instead, you guessed it; I did it up bigger than I had for several years. I put up the tree, decorated it, put out my Santa collection. I decorated the front door. I put up some decorations in almost every room. Okay – every room in the house. I did it all on the first day of November. I was happy. I smiled a lot. I could even smile when I put up the ornaments that I had made for him over the years. The ones that were special from the year we were married the last time. Christmas made me happy. For me, it was filled with good memories.

Surprisingly, I had also been watching Christmas movies since July. I did not have the Hallmark channel since I did not have cable, so I watched them on other channels that I did have. Yes, I cried at some of them. Yes, I missed my husband and his protesting about me watching them for so many months. I usually did not watch them much if he was home. In 2019 I made up for those times I missed watching them. I found myself able to smile. I was able to enjoy them. After a while, they all seemed the same, and by Christmas, I had seen enough. At least until the next year.

November 2, 2019, I started writing my book - number three in the trilogy. I reached the minimum of 50,000 words by the 8th of November. I kept writing until almost the end of the month when the book's rough draft was complete with about 90,000 words. I was thrilled! My three-book trilogy was done. I had written the entire series in one year. Less than one year, considering the time off while my husband was in the hospital and the four months it took for my writing creativity to return. It was time to sit back, relax and enjoy the holiday season.

Thanksgiving for my family was always different than most families. At least for the previous eleven years that I worked retail. The store is open for Black Friday. It was open on Thursday for their 'big' sales for the last several years, and I always worked it because it came with extra benefits. My local family learned to rearrange how we celebrated. The year I became a widow, we changed it more. In years past, we would each make portions of the meal and then gather at my daughter and son-in-law's house to eat. This time, instead of cooking, we all went out to eat the Sunday before Thanksgiving. Since I worked on Thanksgiving, my daughter, son-in-law, grandson, and my son-in-law's parents always planned to go out of town to meet up with more of his side of the family. It worked out perfectly for everyone. There was no reason to change that because of me being alone. I was glad for the change in the meal this time. As much as I was into the holiday season, I was not into cooking this holiday.

On Thanksgiving Day, I was alone before I had to go to work. I watched the parade on TV. I was thankful for all the memories of the Thanksgiving days we had shared in the past. I remembered a few we spent out of town. I remembered Thanksgiving when I was growing up, and the one year it snowed so bad no one could make it to our house on time to eat. I smiled as I remembered the many years I shared with my love. I remembered the first Thanksgiving when my daughter had been born a week before. I remembered the good times I have had in my life. I was thankful. I had been so blessed. I stayed positive. God was with me and gave me the courage to stay strong. I enjoyed the day, alone, at home.

Then, in the middle of the afternoon, I went to work and dealt with Black Friday until midnight. The hardest part that night was going home to an empty house. I know, I had already done it for months. This time was different. On Black Friday, he had always stayed up waiting for me to come home. This time he wasn't going to be there to tell me goodnight while he got up to do his own Black Friday shopping at other stores that were having big sales. This time we were not going to turn around and both go shopping like we had done a few years. This time..... I was going home and going to bed.

Christmas. This was not my first Christmas alone. It was, however, my first as a widow. This year would have some special memories. It was the gifts that were special this year and the time with some of the family. This year we were missing a key member, and it was one we would not forget. I had told the family I wanted to spend most of it alone. They were okay with that. I had been blessed all along this journey that friends nor family insisted I get out and do things. Nor did they insist I spend time with them. They let me choose the way I wanted to handle each day. And this day, I wanted to be mostly alone.

It may seem odd that the first Christmas as a widow was a very special Christmas for me. But a month or so after my husband died, I decided I needed to write his life story. My grandson, who spent at least one day a week with us and had been so close to his Papaw, was my initial inspiration. They had their special time together.

When our grandson was very little, and Papaw came inside, he would follow his Papaw into our bedroom and help him take his shoes off and put them where they belonged. My husband wore a special brace on his foot, and our grandson would help take that off and put it where it belonged next to his shoes. Somehow they started a routine of lying on the bed to have little chats. Our grandson would ask his Papaw to tell him a story. Papaw would ask him what he wanted to hear, and his answer was always, "Tell me about when you were a little boy." Papaw was thrilled to share his stories. After his Papaw died, I knew I had to write his life story. I was never allowed in the room when they had those special moments, so I have no idea what any of those stories were. Whenever I would get close to the room, our grandson would tell me to go away. They were having "Man Talk," he would tell me. After his Papaw died, I asked my grandson if he remembered any of the stories, and he sadly shook his head and quietly said, 'No". I felt bad that he did not remember. I hope someday he will be able to think back, and even though he was very young, I hope he can remember at least their time together.

I began to write my husband's story. Ninety-three pages later, it was complete with plenty of time to print it out and make a copy for each of the children and grandchildren. I knew that it might be years before some of them read it. I also knew that if I did not write it while the memories were fresh in my mind, I would forget some of his stories that I knew. I am sure I forgot to include a lot of what he did in his life; I simply wrote what I remembered and what he had told me over the years. I also included what a few others had shared with me after he died. We were in our early 30's when we met, and each of us had been married before; because of this, I know there are things I never knew about him.

Another special event that first Christmas came through my husband's grandson in Pennsylvania. He told his mom that he wanted the latest cell phone and an old pickup truck to fix up for Christmas. He had not turned 13 yet. His request still touches my heart. His Grandpa (Papaw to some of our grandchildren, Grandpa to others) had a red 1997 GMC pickup truck. It was in my name by then, and I had tried unsuccessfully to sell it. I saw where my stepdaughter posted on Facebook her son's request and instantly knew what I had to do. After my initial tears dried up, I contacted her. I proposed my offer to her. She talked it over with her husband, and they agreed to my offer. So, on Christmas day, our grandson unwrapped a bucket with car cleaner, rags, car wax, and a sponge. He had no clue what that was all for. He kept pulling things out of the bucket. The next thing he pulled out was a framed photo of his grandpa's truck and the spare key I had sent. Let's simply say there were a lot of tears.

The weekend between Christmas and New Year's Day, my stepdaughter and her husband flew down and stayed for a few hours. We all went to our favorite restaurant for lunch with my daughter and her family. Before they left, driving the pickup to their home, I asked my stepdaughter to call me and let me know they had made it home. It's a long story to understand this next comment, and there is no need to explain it. She told me she never had a mother who cared that much for her. I told her she had one now. On their way home, she texted me when they stopped for gas and stopped for the night. Then she texted me the next morning before they left the hotel when they stopped to shop on the way home and again when they did get home. She probably doesn't know how good those texts made me feel. I have been blessed that she and I have developed such a close relationship. Closer now than it has ever been. I am so grateful.

Yes, Christmas that first year, almost seven months after my husband died, was a very special Christmas for me. Christmas day, I went over to my daughter's for breakfast and to open all the gifts. With all the decorations up at my house and all the Christmas music I had listened to and movies I had watched, I still wanted to spend most of the day alone. It was my choice. I needed it. My friends may not have understood it. Even my family may not have understood, but they accepted it and let me be alone.

What will the next Christmas bring? I do not know. I do have the ornaments bought; I have to paint them. Unless I change my mind about what ornaments to give them. Whatever I decide, I hope to have another positive Christmas.

I have several very special ornaments that my sister painted for me over the years, a few I made, new ones from my sister, my stepdaughter, and my grandchildren. I decided to set up a spot in my house to have Christmas all year long. For the time being, it is in my bedroom. I get to see the ornaments that mean the most to me every day. You might say I like Christmas a little.

New Year's Eve. We had always spent that at home, and he always went to bed before midnight. This year I did like I always did. I stayed up and watched the ball drop. I missed him telling me Happy New Year before he went to bed, and I hated that we never got another New Year together. I woke up to a new day, a new year, and realized that the new year would be different for my family and me.

The year continued with several holidays still to get through in a new way – as a widow. Several holidays were ones we never celebrated in any special way. So this year, they were just the same ordinary days as they always had been.

St. Patrick's Day was one of those. I only put up a few decorations every year and leave it at that. No celebrations, no special foods. It was always just another day. This time I put up the decorations and was struck with the significance of the seventeenth of March. I never let it get to me before. It never affected me the way it would now. The root of what led to his death all began on March 17, 2016. A work injury that had led to surgeries, therapies, lost work, pain, and now the knowledge that it had eventually left me a widow. I got through the day with simple sadness. I knew there was nothing I could do to change any of it.

Life is all about how we deal with what we are handed. I do my best to take it all in a positive light. To be happy with my decisions. To enjoy family and friends and even to enjoy my time alone. Time to be creative and share my stories.

Easter was another holiday we never celebrated more than sunrise service together for several years. We had no little kids to help color Easter eggs and hide them. My fond memories of Easter come more in memories of my father. I will always remember the Easters Daddy would give my mother a tulip plant. He always bought one for his mother and my Mom's mother. One year when I was maybe sixteen, he bought me one as well. I was honored. I never told my husband about that, as I did not want him to do that for me. To me, that was something special between my Dad and me. So this Easter was another ordinary day for me. Due to what was taking place in the country and the world with the Coronavirus, I stayed home in a quiet house. My connection to others was through Facebook and a few texts. The weather was chilly, windy, and rainy, with a bad storm headed my way overnight.

Mother's Day without him was not so bad. I joined my daughter, son-in-law, grandson, and the 'out-laws' for a mid-morning breakfast and a short visit. The kids had to go car shopping since my daughter had been in a minor car accident that totaled her car and only had a week to find a new car. I was fine with not spending a lot of time there. I am finding more and more comfort in staying at home and doing my own thing. I am not sure if that is a good thing or a bad thing in the overall scheme of things, but, for me, it is a good thing as it gives me time to think, dream, be creative, and write.

May 14th. A very special day in my life. I was married on this day - twice. And this year would have been our twenty-sixth and/or our fifteenth wedding anniversary. I knew early in my journey of grief what I wanted to do today if the weather permitted. When our country got hit with the Coronavirus, and even the parks were closed, I was not sure I would be able to go where I wanted to. They opened up in time, and a girlfriend and I made the trip I wanted to make to Roan Mountain, Tennessee. We visited the site where my husband and I got married the last time and where his ashes are scattered. We enjoyed the beauty of the area, and I took over three hundred photos of our day. On the way home we stopped to pick up food from his favorite restaurant, which we ate at my home.

I did not cry until later in the day, and then I only shed a few tears. Overall I smiled and even laughed. I was touched by everyone who commented on the photos I posted and sent me their love and virtual hugs. That meant a lot to me.

Yes, it was a very special day for me. Even more so, I think, because since he is gone, I had the honor of remembering him and the life we had, the weddings we had, and the joy we had over the years we shared.

Chapter Eleven

One Year - I Made It

When I reached the nine-month anniversary, I felt I was doing good. It was at that time that I decided to write this book. I knew if I could make it through my grief, so could others.

I had taken care of all the legal things I needed to handle. I had bought myself new things, including a newer car. I was getting things together to have a second yard sale. I was planning a long trip to see my family out of state. I was getting through entire weeks without shedding so many tears. Most of the time, when I felt emotional and teared up, it was without a down-and-out crying session.

At nine months, I was feeling good about how far I had come. I still had a few goals to reach within my first year. These, as I wrote about in the previous chapter, were put on hold to no fault of my own. I will reach them as soon as possible - when we as a country can move around, travel, and be close to others again.

There are some things I have to do or have someone do for me around the house this summer. I will get them done. It is part of my determination to accomplish this and get them done as soon as possible to simply move on with my life. I will get there.

There were times, leading up to the first nine months, that I knew I was further along my path than some who were a year or more in their grieving. I am not sure why. Maybe it is part of my belief that life happens, and so does death. Some people thrive; some are still in so much pain they can't get through the day.

I woke up one morning in the middle of April and realized that it had been eleven months since I had been able to hear his voice, feel his hug, and see the love in his eyes. I suddenly had the realization that although his actual death was June 1, 2019. I had lost him on the nineteenth of May. He still had me with him until the first of June, even though I had lost the person he was. So my first year of survival started in the middle of May. I think my grieving started then as well. It certainly started when the doctor told me he would never recover, and we had to make that unbelievable decision to let him go. That was the beginning of the end, the beginning of a new way of living for me, his family, and his friends.

May arrived and with it a sense of accomplishment. I found myself strong, positive, capable, even smiling, and happy. I began to laugh more. I could sit and watch TV shows and movies that dealt with families losing loved ones. I could read a book or a few pages from a book that dealt with a husband dying and not be overcome by tears or sadness. I did pay attention to how the actors portrayed their emotions after experiencing their loss and could understand or disagree with the writers. I could listen to songs that had made me cry but now smile while I felt the emotions they convey. They were filled with love. A love I could now appreciate and feel in a positive imaginary hug.

I had reached a point of knowing I was going to be okay. That I already was okay. That I not only could survive, but I was also making it on my own. I was becoming Me. I was, I am, I will continue to be a new ME.

When I celebrated my wedding anniversary by going to the mountain with a dear friend, I posted on Facebook about my trip, shared photos, and raised a toast to my love.

Comments came with love, hugs, emojis of tears. And a few of 'I know you're having a bad day,' or 'I feel your pain,' 'I know the heartache.' I was not having a bad day. I was not in pain. I was not feeling the heartache I once had. I was having a wonderful day. I was laughing, smiling, and enjoying my new life while celebrating what would have been our anniversary.

Three days after what had been our wedding anniversary, I faced the first anniversary of my husband's surgery. I awoke before the alarm. The alarm that I set every day, even on the days I did not have to get up. I wanted to be sure not to oversleep. I always set the alarm for early in the morning. On May 17th, I set it for 5:30 AM. I woke up at 5 AM, ready to face the day. I wrote a bit about how I felt about the day in relation to a year ago. I chatted online with a few people. I called his sister.

Each conversation was a good positive conversation. None had any tears. Life was moving forward for all of us. My stepdaughter told me she took a walk and cried a lot during that time. I wish I could have been there to hold her. I was 500 miles away during a pandemic and could not travel there. The rest of the day simply progressed into a very long day. I had things I wanted to do but never did. There is always another day; although I know too well, there may not always be a next day. And so, I ended that day and journeyed on to the anniversary of the day he coded. That was the day, in my mind, that I lost the love of my life.

With anticipation, I waited. I wondered. Could I face the day a year later? Could I get up and go about my day normally? Would I choose to hide within the walls of my home, hidden underneath the blankets for protection against reality? Would I be able to sleep the night before? Would I relive the moments that occupied the 24-36 hours around the time I lost my soulmate? That moment when the life he knew and loved was suddenly stopped for three minutes, after which he never responded to those he loved again.

Knowing there was nothing I could do to change anything about one year ago, I fought the possibility of tears. I fought to stay strong. I fought to stay positive and keep going. I sensed my late husband telling me, as he often did, go on, go to work, you can do it, I'll be okay. Yes, he is okay. And yes, I would go on with my day and my life.

May 19, 2019. The day he coded. A day I reflected on a year later. -- Another day in my life that will live with me forever. I can picture it clearly in my mind and think back to things I wished I would have done differently. Then I look back on my life with my love and how he always would tell me not to worry about him and do what I was going to do. The evening of the eighteenth that year was no different. I should have spent the night. Instead, he told me to go home, get some rest, and take care of Abby, our German Shepherd. He told me he would see me in the morning and to take my time coming in, not to rush. He told me he was not going anywhere. So, like I had done most of our life together, I did exactly what he wanted me to do. I went home. I took care of Abby. I rested (maybe that was a good thing). I also decided to sleep in a bit because I figured all would be well and he would be coming home that day. Instead, I got a call that he was having trouble breathing, and they had moved him to another room. That was all the nurse told me on the phone when she called. I told her I would be in shortly. I still had to walk our dog and feed her. I took care of Abby's needs and was headed to the hospital when I got another call from another nurse. This one said that they had moved him again. I told the nurse that I was on my way. When I got to the room he was supposed to be in, the nurse met me in the hall and told me that he had coded. You know that time in your life when you hear a certain word, and after that the world goes silent? You don't hear another word before you interrupt the person speaking? Yes, that moment. I stopped him in mid-sentence. No one had told me he had coded until him. He could not believe it. Fast forward an hour or so. I was meeting with three specialists. I only heard a part of what they were telling me. He had coded for about 3 minutes; they got him back, they were unsure if there was any brain damage. Again – shock. I took a deep breath. After the two specialists left, the critical care doctor stayed and told me more, and in terms I could understand. Then she took me in to see the love of my life. She warned me what he would look like with all the tubes and wires. I had seen those before on others and was prepared for that. I was not prepared for the next twelve days. I faced the day alone. I called his daughter and his sister to tell them what was going on. I called my daughter. I handled the day on my own and went home late in the day.

The next day I called his sister and agreed that she should come and stay with me. She was a Godsend.

Yes, on the nineteenth - the first anniversary, I relived all those moments as if they were currently happening. I probably always will.

It was the same a few days later on the anniversary of surgery two and three—a thirty-six-hour stretch of no sleep a year ago. I can still feel the pain. I can envision sitting in the waiting room through the entire nine hours of his surgery - waiting, praying, crying, doing my best to be strong. Worried. Hoping.

To no avail. There was not only an improvement; it was worse. It continued to be the ending.

A week later, One doctor told me there was no hope. My husband would never recover. I can still remember standing there listening to the only doctor who was willing to tell me the truth—the only doctor with balls enough to be honest and give me the facts at that moment.

I thought the nineteenth was going to be rough this year. I was fine. It was the twenty-second that got me.

We never know what days or what triggers will set off the flood of tears. We can do our best to be strong and keep the tears at bay. We can stay positive all we want. We can take steps to move forward as far and as fast as we work ourselves and our minds to go. There are no rules to the time frame. There are also no rules or time frame when you wake up one day, and the tears are cascading, and there is no stopping them. We learn to let them flow. The sun will shine again. The rainbow will form and land in your heart again. For the time being, the tears are there – let them flow. Let the day take over. Reach out to someone to hold on to and cry on their shoulder. Write out your thoughts. Go for a drive.

I wrote; I went for a drive; I cried; I looked at the clouds in the sky a Lot. I talked to the cardinal that landed on the wire at the power pole outside my window. Then it flew away. I smiled at the bluebird that graced my view a few times during the day. I smiled and said, "Thanks, Mom," to the Yellow Swallowtail butterfly that flew by while I was on my drive. It was a day filled with reminders of loved ones I had lost in my life. It was a day that began with wishing I could talk to my mom and tell her all that I had been through and how much I had accomplished in my life since she had passed thirty years before. I wanted to share with her that I had finally made it, and I was proud of my accomplishments. Then it occurred to me that many of the things I considered successes had come because of my suffering. I would not be where I was without losing my soulmate. After thinking back over the year, shedding a few tears and smiles, the day ended with me considering myself a survivor. I Had made it. I had made it a year on my own. I had survived. The sun did come out again. Figuratively and literally. God is good. He is always there with us. He will carry me through. He will carry you through it as well.

I did not have anyone I wanted to call to lean on while I cried that day. I did not want anyone to come over to lend me their shoulder. I wanted to be left alone. I wanted the time to cry. I needed the time to talk to God, to share with Him my feelings. I needed to cleanse my soul.

So, at the end of the day, seeing the blue sky and the sun peek past the clouds and clear away the rain, I knew God had also taken the day to give me tears (my rain) to cleanse my soul. My thoughts. My clouds. He gave me a chance to feel the presence of my soulmate, who I could hear telling me it was again okay to move forward. To feel my mother giving me her blessing as she often does. It was my time to know that what is past is past. It can not be changed. We can learn from it. We can cherish the wonderful moments. We can even cherish the sad moments and know that God was with us through it all.

June 1. One year! Suddenly that day arrived, and I wondered how time had gone by so fast. I knew it was coming. The days and weeks went slow as I counted each one. The months slowly counted off their numbers. Then the first anniversary of the day my soulmate died arrived. The year had gone quickly. I anticipated how I was going to handle the day. Would I cry all day? Should I cry all day? Would I hide in my house? Stay in bed? Feel sorry for myself? Be angry? I had managed all the days, months, holidays, events, and living so far. Would I manage to get through this day?

There was no crying, no hiding in my house, no staying in bed, no feeling sorry for myself, no anger. No. I got up early and headed out on my first ever on-my-own road trip. It was only an hour away and turned into a destination and day I enjoyed. I followed that with a stop in my little town and took a walk. I was always traveling with my camera; I took over 250 photos of my adventures at day's end. I found peace along the way. I saw God's blessings. I felt comfort and found more strength. I felt ready to face year two.

One year. It had been a year of many changes. Changes that I made on my own. Changes that the world made for me during this time. Changes that God saw me through. Changes that made me stronger. Changes that allowed me to be weak when I needed to be, followed by God lifting me when it was time. Changes that pushed me to be a new person. Changes that will follow me for the rest of my life. Changes, growth, and living showed me I had made it. Yes, I had made it.

I still have several things I want to take care of and change. Achieving my goals was interrupted by the pandemic; however, my growth and mental changes continued. My goals will be reached at some point. The weather will warm up, and people will be back to work, traveling, and enjoying life. I will be able to travel again; I will have the yard sale I wanted to have. I will be able to sell or get rid of things that I do not want to keep and make my life what it now is - My life.

My life, at one year, was very good. I was blessed. I was looking forward.

I was ready to face the rest of my life.

Chapter Twelve

I Understand

Not everyone grieves the same. Our circumstances are different. Our love relationships are different. We go through the stages of grief at different times. We have different family structures. Our friends are different. Yet, we all grieve and always will. We all feel the pain. We all have a heart that aches so bad you can feel the physical pain inside. A pain that no medication can touch.

I know some suffer from grief to the point of not knowing how they will even get out of bed each day. Some don't want to move anything in their home that belonged to their loved one. Some don't know how to cope with life, living, working, or being on their own. I understand.

During my first year of grieving, I came to understand that not every widow or widower I met would become a new friend. While there was the bond of grieving that we shared, that was as far as the connection went. I had people who were there to help me through my days and my emotions telling me I was normal. Some were telling me I was already beyond where they were. We were there for each other to help get through a moment of time in our lives. Our common interests beyond that did not hold us together. At first, that bothered me. Then as I became the one that others leaned on, instead of me leaning on others, I realized that it was not required that I stay a part of their lives for any longer than they needed me, as it was not their job to be there for me for any longer than I needed them. I was always there for them when they needed me, and I was fine when that time ended. When they did not need me, I knew they were doing better independently—surviving and hopefully thriving. Or that they were leaning on someone else who could give them what they needed during the stage they were experiencing. I was grateful to have several ladies who were there for me as I needed them. To be the shoulder I needed to get through the very beginning and the rough days I had throughout the first year. I was also grateful when those who leaned on me could step out independently and not need me as often.

As you have read through how I handled my first year, I hope it has helped you. I hope you have seen by my experience that it can be done. You can get through this time in your life and do it positively.

Accept that there will be rough days even when you do your best to stay positive and try not to let the tears fall, and the sadness brings you down. You will always have those moments. It is part of the never-ending grieving of the person you loved and still love after they are gone. I still grieve the loss of my father, who died in 1979, and my mother, who died in 1990. Both were so young when they died. I miss them. I wish I could still have a conversation with them. I wish -- a lot of things. I miss my grandparents. I miss a lot of people who have died that had played a part in my life. Some days I shed tears for them as well. I will always miss my husband and wish he were still here to talk with, laugh with and share my life with, but I know the only conversations with him will be in my thoughts. My writing is my way of sharing him and our love with everyone. This book of my positive journey is my way of sharing and helping you travel your journey.

Whether you are a new widow or widower, have been one for many years and have already moved forward, or are still stuck and can't seem to take any steps forward, I hope this book and my story, as well as the pages that follow, will help you in your journey. I hope you have someone you can lean on when you need them. I hope you are there when someone needs to lean on you.

As I start my second year, I face it head-on. I hope and pray it is an easier year overall. I hope another pandemic does not hit and interrupt my plans. I hope this first one soon leaves. I hope and pray I can be there for those who reach out to me for encouragement and guidance. I have no idea if this book will be a success or if only a few people will read it. That does not matter. What matters is for those who read it that it touches your heart and helps you prepare and heal.

Be an encouragement. Stay positive. Find the new you. May God bless you.

PHYLLIS DEWEY/HER TURN

Epilogue

What is Next?

(Written soon after the first anniversary of my husband's death)

I can honestly say I do not know what is next for me. For now, it is to live each day to the best that I can with God's help. My plans and His may differ. I will continue to lean on Him each and every day.

I know what my plans and goals are. I have places I want to go and people I want to see. I hope to get stronger and braver each day. I accept that there may be setbacks. I understand that some days, weeks, even months may still be difficult to face. I realize the least little thing could bring a smile, a laugh, a tear, or an out and out down-pouring of tears. I also realize that as prepared as I feel, I will occasionally be surprised and shocked at how life moving forward and the memories of a cherished life with him will affect me.

I know there are things my spouse and I should have done differently while we were married. Having a will, having a living will, saving more money, being out of debt. A better relationship at times. All of these things fall under the 'should haves' that go along with those 'what ifs.' It's too late for any of them. The knowledge gained from them can be put into my future.

My plans? My goals? Writing. Writing has been my passion since I was a child. I plan to write, to do my best to become published. I want to be able to retire and live the life God wants me to live. I want to be there for others who are going through the things I have been through during my life.

Losing my husband is just one of the life events I have experienced. What are the others? Divorce. Spousal Abuse. Moving to a state where I only knew two other people who lived there and calling it my home years later. Having children. Life without my children living with me and being a stepmother. They all are the experiences making up the stories that make me who I am. They each are their own story. Each one I faced. Each one I made it through. Each one added to the *me* that you, my readers, are now getting to know.

So what does my future hold? What is my 'epilogue' to all this? Life continues for me, and it will continue for you as well. We get through it. We face all our fears. We are strong. We learn to take one step at a time, one breath at a time, and eventually, we are breathing normally again as we face our new life and love the new person we become.

Keep breathing.
       Keep taking those steps.
              Keep moving forward.

Epilogue #2

Year Two

(Written twenty-one months after my husband's death)

I wrote this book during and immediately following the first year after my husband died. At that time, I did not know what I would be doing during the months leading up to the second anniversary.

As I now get closer to that day, I look back over the last several months and know I have made great strides forward – again.

The Covid-19 Pandemic occupied all of those months, but I did not let that stop me in my tracks. Instead, I used it to keep moving forward in my life and my living.

After June 1, 2020, I was keeping myself busy with work and writing. In October, I told myself I had had enough of staying at home. Some travel restrictions were lifted, and I headed north to Pennsylvania. I visited with my son, granddaughter, bonus daughter, family, and then further North to visit with my sister, brother-in-law, and some other family I had not seen in about six years! I drove the eight hours up with only one stop. I then went two hours further north to see my sister and then a ten-hour trip home, taking only time for two quick stops. All on my own! Yes – accomplishment! I was proud of myself. And it was one thing to mark off my list of things I wanted to do.

The fall held more holidays to celebrate without my husband. This time they were easier to enjoy. Thanksgiving was held at my house with my daughter, son-in-law, and grandson. After dinner, we watched a movie together.

Christmas Day, I went over to their home for breakfast, then later, they came over to mine to open gifts. My son and granddaughter were going to come down from Pennsylvania, but they decided to wait until July of 2021 to visit due to the pandemic. So I left the small Christmas tree up in the den along with all their gifts until they visit in July.

I was able to have my back deck railing and stairs replaced in December.

Then 2021 arrived, and with it, some great changes in my life! Some planned, one not planned.

In January, I achieved the goal of becoming a published author when *Leaving Came Easy, The Mysteries of Bella Rose Estate, Book One* was published and available on Amazon.com. In just over a month, I had sixty-five books sold and ten that I gave to family and a couple of close friends. I had a book signing event in February that I had not even thought of having but, that worked out great. The country was still dealing with the pandemic, but we could have people come out and buy an autographed copy of my book. Goals for the rest of the year are to publish four more books; this book is one of those.

In February, I had the roof replaced on my house. Now I would not have to worry about that causing issues.

The one thing that I had not planned on was meeting someone new that brought unexpected smiles and happiness into my life. I had not been looking. I had planned to live out the rest of my life alone, by choice, and I was happy with the way my life was going. One day, during a conversation with a friend, he asked me if I would like to have dinner with him sometime. After initially and immediately saying, "No," we started to get to know each other through texts, phone calls, and short in-person conversations. The next time he asked, I said, 'Yes,". And I am so glad I did.

I was concerned about telling my bonus daughter that I was seeing someone new after her father died. When I told her about him, her one comment was, "Just as long as he knows you are a package deal.... You, your daughter, your son, and me! She spoke the truth; I am a package deal, take it or leave it. My family will always be my life. He knew this and agreed. He came as a package too. He even told me to stop calling her my bonus daughter; she was my daughter. That is so true; she may not be my blood daughter, but we are close, and I consider her my daughter.

I may not know how my life will be a year from now. I may not know what it will be like a month from now. I do know – I am happy. Happier than I thought I ever would be or planned to be. I found there was room in my life and in my heart for you, happiness, and yes I know in time there will be room for love again.

For those widows and widowers who think, as I did, that there will never be another love like you just lost—never say never. I agree that there will never be another mate like the one you lost. Each person is different. Each person comes with a past. Each person comes as a package, as my one daughter says.
Nothing says that those who have lost their spouse should look for a new love in their lives. In the same sense, nothing says it cannot happen. And if or when it happens, I wish joy and happiness for you.

Part 2

Helping You Through Your Journey

PHYLLIS DEWEY/HER TURN

Introduction

Death. We all face it. We all lose someone we love. Whether it be a grandparent, parent, spouse, child, another relative, or a friend, we eventually face death. We mourn, and then we grieve. It is the natural response.

Even cows grieve. I've watched them grieve for a week after losing a baby calf. For a solid week, each morning a group of cows gathered at the spot where a calf died. They formed a circle, lowered their heads, were quiet, and stood there for several minutes before moving away and going about the rest of their day. The next day at the same time, they were there again. After a week, they did not gather anymore. Their time of mourning and grieving was over. Do cows remember that loss after that week and continue to grieve? I have no idea. I know we humans do.

We all grieve in our own way, through our own timing. Grieving is normal. However you grieve, it is normal. Do not ever let anyone tell you how to grieve. Do not let anyone tell you that you should be past grieving in a certain amount of time. Years later, you will still grieve. You will always miss the person who died. The intensity lessens over time, and the grieving moments do not last as long. Ask anyone; grieving does not end.

My father died in 1979. I still miss him. I still shed a tear for him from time to time. I miss my grandparents, my mother, several of my friends. I have not let any of those losses keep me down. A setback from time to time, yes. Quiet moments as I remember them and the joy they brought to my life, yes. Quiet talks to them from time to time, yes. I learned early on that life goes on, and I have to let it. I cannot stop living.

I wrote this Part Two to give you an insight into what to expect, things to take care of, and how to prepare some things ahead of time to make living after losing a loved one easier.

Use the next part of this book as a reference and a learning tool. A lot of what I share can be found on the internet if you look. There are things that I may not have included that you will be able to find on your own through the internet or books. Feel free to make notes along the way for things that relate to your needs and your life. And to add things you find on your own. This book is for you.

This book is geared to deal with the loss of your spouse. I relate it to a husband's death, as the widow who grieves and lives life afterward. A lot of what I discuss can be related to any loved one you have lost. Feel free to interpret my usage of the term *widow* to however it best fits in your life.

Chapter One

Stages and Emotions of Grief

There are several stages of grief. If you look up 'Stages of Grief' on the internet, you will see various numbers of stages and explanations for them. Below I list and discuss seven stages of grief. I will share how I was affected by the ones I experienced and then give you my thoughts on ways you may find helpful to deal with them.

Understand that you do not have to go through every stage in your grieving process. You may go through some of them more than once. You do not have to go through them in any specific order.

In the beginning, grieving is hard. You think you will never stop crying. You feel like a basket case over your loss. You wonder if what you are feeling is normal. You think it should be easier. In time it will get better. Know that you will always grieve. You will always miss that person. You will always have rough moments. The rough days, weeks, and months will get better. Remember that it is okay to grieve – your way, your timing. Do not let it control your life and keep you down. We do not grieve for a short time and *get over it*. We grieve – for the rest of our lives to some degree. We learn to move forward. We learn there is still life to live. Getting there is possible.

THE STAGES –

Here are the seven stages I will discuss: Remember, you will find others or variations to these on the internet, in books, and discussed by others. These are what best fit into my life.

1. SHOCK AND DENIAL
2. PAIN AND GUILT
3. ANGER AND RAGE
4. DEPRESSION, LONELINESS, AND REFLECTION
5. UPWARD TURN
6. WORKING THROUGH IT AND RECONSTRUCTION
7. ACCEPTANCE

Grieving encompasses more than the known stages of grief. There are emotions that go along with and intertwine with those stages of grief we experience.

Stages and Emotions! All of them. Some of them. All at once. One at a time. Repeatedly. Over time. Your time. It doesn't matter if you were prepared for the death of your loved one like I briefly was, or if it was sudden. You will go through so many emotions over time that sometimes you wonder if you will ever be normal. You will wonder if they will ever go away. All those thoughts are normal. You will be okay. You will begin to wonder if you ever had a life without feeling some of them. Then one day, you will realize you are okay. You will smile again. You have gotten through. You will laugh. You will be happy.

I was able to experience all of these stages in a short amount of time and all on my own. I never sought out professional help. At the beginning of my grieving process, one person I talked with suggested I seek a therapist or a grieving group to help deal with it. In our conversation, I told her that my college degree was in social work/mental health. "Oh, you'll be fine then. You can handle this." Her comment made me think and smile later. I guess I took her words to heart. I was able to handle it. From what a lot of people have told me, I did it quite well. That is also why I wanted to write this book, to help others go through it and know that it is possible to come out on the other side a new person.

You may want or need to seek help. A grief group, individual counseling, group counseling, or at least a Facebook group or two with like-minded people may be to your benefit. To connect with someone who has gone through it or is going through it is helpful. I belong to three Facebook groups that deal with grief. I did not spend a lot of time on the one because it made me feel worse than I already did. By the time I found them, I was already moving forward. The group members were still in the initial stages of pain, anger, depression, and loneliness. I was already working through it with acceptance and hope. I was planning ahead. While it helped to know I was not alone, it was not what I needed at that time. I stay in the group to encourage others, always being mindful that I do not fall back into my deep grief. For those who have taken that deep breath and are ready to move forward, it is better to find a group that is moving forward. Find one that fits where you are in your grief and where you are headed. If you feel you do not fit in a particular group, whether it be on Facebook or in person, know that it is okay to quit and find a better source of help. Find what works for you. I also encourage others to do their best to stay away from medications. While the medications may help ease the pain, help you sleep, and help you function each day, I caution you not to get hooked on them. Do your best to rely on being positive, looking forward, finding happiness, and finding You.

In part one of this book, you read my overall story. Here are the stages and emotions as I dealt with them and how you may get through them.

SHOCK

Shock came to me not because it was a sudden, unexpected death. I knew it was coming, and I knew roughly when it was coming. The shock for me was the instant he took his last breath, and I knew it was over. I was shocked by the realization of simply being in shock. I had dealt with the death of loved ones before. I had been there when other relatives had taken their last breath. I thought I was prepared for it. I was not. I cannot describe how I felt other than Numb, just plain numb. When he took his last breath I remember waiting a few seconds wanting him to take one more breath. One more inhale. I held my breath, hoping he would take another one. There was no more. He was gone. I stood there holding his hand, crying, looking around at the close family gathered by his side holding his hands. I watched as their tears fell. I felt my tears fall. I refused to fall apart. I felt I had to be the strong one for them. My son, my daughter, his daughter and son-in-law, his sister, and his niece; they were there. For him. For me. Yet, I felt I was the one who should hold everyone else together. I was finally able to let go of his hand and step back. I sat down. I cried while they continued to stand by his side. Between my tears I watched them. I saw their love for him pour out to him. I then attempted to stand up, immediately falling back into my chair. My feet would not hold me up. Yes, I was in shock.

Shock may hit you in the beginning as it hit me. It hits hard when the death is unexpected. It hits hard when you know it is eventually coming. It is hard to handle. Your mind goes blank. Your thoughts go back to try to remember the last time you said, "I love you." Your mind races to so many things at once you can not make sense of any of it. The shock could leave in a few minutes. It could last a lot longer. I believe when their death is unexpected and sudden, the shock may last longer. It also may return from time to time. The shock will wear off over time.

DENIAL

I believe we all go through this. I would come home from work and expect him to be sitting on the couch waiting for me. At work, I would look for him to show up while he was shopping and stop by to say hello. I knew full well that he was gone, and the thoughts of him actually greeting me when I went home at that point freaked me out some. For some reason, I decided to give my house a name. That way, when I entered the house, I could call out her name and say hello to my house. It worked. 'Matilda' and I are doing fine.

You may spend a longer period of time in denial. You may experience denial in such a profound way that it is unhealthy.

Some ways to describe denial is the inability to face and accept the truth; denying the other person is gone; unable to move forward; refusing to move anything in the house that belonged to the other person; continuing to speak of the other person in the present tense; believing they will return home; refusing to allow anyone to say your loved one has died.

Denial, for a while, is normal. When it interferes with day-to-day living life and your ability to move forward, it is time to seek help.

PAIN AND GUILT

This one comes and goes for me. The pain is the heartache I felt so deeply; it was physical pain. Throughout my first year, that pain would resurface from time to time. The loss hurts; physically hurts, and I cannot explain why nor how. It is more than an empty feeling. His death left a hole in my heart. That hole felt like a literal hole that could not be sewn back together. The pain of that hole hurt to the core of my being. It is a feeling that everything inside you has been taken out with nothing left inside except space, a space where love filled your soul.

My guilt is the 'what if.' What if a different doctor did his surgery? What if he had waited one more day? What if it was a different medical team? What if he and I had decided not to have the surgery at all. Once in a great while, I even thought, 'what if I had not given the okay to disconnect the support that kept him breathing. What if, What if, What if. The list could go on. The what-ifs only caused pain, and I knew there was nothing I could do to change the past. What happened, for whatever reason, happened.

The pain you will feel is a feeling no one can explain to you. It hurts like hell. It is a physical pain that pain medication cannot touch. It is a feeling no one understands until they go through it. It hurts to take a deep breath. It HURTS, period! You will get through it.

The guilt felt will be different for each person reading this. I think most who have lost a spouse feel guilty in some way. You may feel guilty that they died and you are still here. You may feel it because you believe you feel their death was your fault. You may feel it because you were the one who decided to disconnect the life support. You may feel it because you feel there was something more you could have done. You may feel it for any number of reasons. It is normal. However, do NOT let guilt rule your day, week, month, year, or life.

I won't say, 'Get over it.' I will tell you that spending precious hours reliving and thinking back with 'what ifs' is NOT helping you, nor will it bring them back—the 'What-ifs' will get you down and keep you down if you let them. The sooner you can accept whatever happened in your situation, the better you will feel. It may seem impossible to do in the beginning. And it will take some people longer than others to get to that stage. Over time, and when you look back, you will see that it helped you in your journey. I will also tell you that even years later, you will occasionally look back and say, "But, What if'? And you will realize there is nothing you can change about what is and what was.

ANGER

Anger for me came in how I initially felt towards the doctors involved. The surgery had a complication. At first, the family and I tried to blame the doctor; then, we did not know who to blame. I still do not know whose fault it was and will most likely never know. It could be no one's fault. I was also angry with someone when they did something they should not have done and later did something else they had no authority to do. My family and I dealt with that person the moment we noticed. I hope none of you have to deal with what I did, although I know some of you will be dealing with a lot more and a lot of different things in your circumstances. Many of them may be worse.

Anger for you may last a lot longer than mine did and be for so many reasons. You may feel angry that they left you, angry that you now have to handle everything on your own, angry that they left you with no money, or deep in debt. You may be angry that your kids or stepkids are fighting over everything, angry that there was no will.

Your anger could be aimed at yourself to a certain degree because you do not know how to do any of the things they used to do. You may become angry that you need to move or have someone move in with you to help pay the bills. Angry …. Angry... there are so many things you could be angry about if you let them. Take your time to feel that anger. Take control of the issues you can change as soon as you can. Enlist someone else who can help you deal with situations that you cannot solve alone. Then raise your head, hold your shoulders back, and take your first step in taking care of Yourself. Take control of your circumstances. You are stronger than you think. Do not let that anger tear your soul apart. Write down what you are angry about and what, if anything, you can do to heal that anger. Anger does you no good. You have living to do. Do not waste living and being happy again on things that eat at you and make life miserable.

RAGE

Rage grabbed me only once. I remember the occurrence like a powerful scene from a movie. I had gone to bed, and as it was my habit after he died, I looked over at his photo by my bed and said, "Good night, Babe." Then I broke out in tears, formed a tight fist, and hit the crap out of his side of the bed and pillow. I was angry that he was no longer there to say good night back to me. That was the only time rage hit me. A brief ten, maybe fifteen minutes. Then I took a deep breath, rolled over, and cried myself to sleep. In the morning, I looked at his photo and told him I was sorry for hitting him.

Rage for you may also be a one-time episode of lashing out. It may happen more often. Be aware of how you are acting and reacting. Do your best to stay in check with your emotions of anger and rage. If you look back and wonder why or how you could have reacted in such a way, know that you were normal. It may be a new emotional and physical reaction for you. Dealing with the death of your spouse will bring on emotions you never had before or in depths you never knew possible. Do your best to control the intensity of your rage. If you find that it is happening more than it should, please seek help dealing with it. There are people that can help you. Take a deep breath and stay calm.

IRRITABILITY

I hope if I was irritable with anyone, they have already forgiven me. I do my best, even on a normal day, not to be irritable. If something upsets me, I will generally keep it to myself. I do have a few friends I confide in that help by allowing me to vent. They are my sounding boards. They take me as I am, letting me vent, and then we all pick up where we were before and go on with life and living.

This stage comes and goes. Like hormones, even little things can make you irritable. It is best if those around you, especially your family, understand your reactions. They may be doing what they think is best for you when in reality, it is not what you want at that moment. You may get upset with the people you have to deal with during this time: the banker, life insurance people, even the funeral home director. Learn to take a deep breath and step back from the moment. Those who understand your situation will have the patience to handle you and your reactions. It helps to have someone you can confide in to be a sounding board. Someone you can tell everything to that won't judge you. At one time in your life, that person was most likely the person who is now gone.

DESPAIR

I never lost hope during my grieving. I hung on to my faith. I had people who were there for me when I needed something done. For things I could not do myself, I knew who to call. I did not feel isolated while being alone. I never felt like I could not take another day of living. I always had a reason to get up in the morning. I never spent the day unable to get out of bed. I will admit there were days I rarely left the sofa. I spent several hours watching TV shows or movies, staring out the window, watching the rain, praying, or taking a nap. I was always up, dressed, and ready to face the day and accepted that some days were meant to be used to relax, think, cry, plan and look back on as another day of survival. Those were the days of God getting me through when I had no energy to take a step outside. I never missed a day of work, an appointment, or an adventure I had previously planned. It was like God knew what days I needed to be still and listen to Him. There is always a reason for each day.

Do the best you can to hang on to hope. You will get through this time in your life. Think back through your life and everything you have been through. Most of you reading this have been through a lot. You have been through hardships. You have been through difficult times in your life. This may be the first time you had to face things independently, which feels so difficult. You may feel that no one is there for you. No one is there to help you. For some of you, even those who said they would be there for you no longer are. Your friends you had as a couple are no longer inviting you to join them. Don't lose hope. Don't give up. There is light at the end of the tunnel. I hope your tunnel is a short one to get through.

If you find yourself alone and feel that no one cares if you do not have anyone who calls or returns your calls, texts, or Facebook chat messages, seek out groups that are there for you. Talk to your counselor or in your grieving group. It may not be easy to reach out to anyone. Check at the end of this book for places to reach out for help.

REGRET

I held on to a few regrets—one being that we did not have more time together in general. I counted my blessings that we had gone on a cruise and taken another shorter trip before my late husband's surgery. We had home projects I wanted to get done. Instead, we took trips. Now I am so glad we did. Other regrets include things that I cannot go back and change anyway. I have been able to let those feelings go. I look back on the few months before my husband died and wonder if subconsciously he knew. He may not have cognitively known it, but I know God knew and believe God made things happen beforehand. I look back and remember comments my husband made or things he tried to show me how to do for what he referred to as 'just in case.'

My other regret was that for years he would tell me stories of his life, and I would tell him he needed to write them down or even write a book of them. He would tell me he was not the writer - I was. I regret we never took the time out of our busy lives to write them down. In the end, as you read in part one, I wrote about his life the best I could, knowing I missed a lot. I wrote it in my words, not his. I think it would have been written differently if it were in his words, even if I had been the one to write them as he spoke them.

Regrets, yes, I have a few, like those 'what ifs,' I cannot change what did or did not happen in the past. I can, however, move forward and change my future. I can advise people to live life, enjoy all the moments. Find and do what you love. Make great memories.

Your regret may be one of wishing you had said. "I love you," more often, or at least that one last time. You may have had a spat, and it was the last thing that happened between the two of you. You may regret a lot of things you now think you would have changed about your life together. Understand that you cannot change anything you may now regret. It is now time to do your best not to regret other things in your life and how you live your future. Change what you can of your future and your life so that you, your family, your loved ones, do not have regrets.

ANXIETY

I was anxious during the time my husband was in the hospital and right after his death. I was anxious about the future, his recovery from the condition he was in, his treatment, and why more was not being done. I was anxious about how life would be for him since, at one time, the 'good news' was that he would need more surgeries, that he would be in more pain instead of less, and that he would not regain his strength. Yes, that was the possible *good* news. I was anxious about him becoming depressed. I was anxious about keeping my job and being without an income. I knew even with the possible good news, he would never be able to do the physical work he had once enjoyed again. My employer held my job for me, for which I am grateful.

After his death, I was anxious about getting everything done when I needed to and making sure I handled everything. And that I handled it correctly. I worried that I would forget something or someone. Since my husband did not have a will, I worried about how all the legal issues would be handled. I was anxious about being able to stay in the house that I loved. That my car would stay running, that everything would not fall apart in my life. I was blessed that everything went smoothly for me. I was blessed with the right people at the right time to see my concerns and be there for me.

All of my anxiety was complicated by my own recently diagnosed medical issue that is triggered by stress. While being anxious, I was also trying to lessen its effects on my health.

You may be anxious about many things that you will have to face after your loved one dies. To help get a grip on those things that worry you, write them down so you can see them. To see them written out, you may be able to face them better. You can envision them. It is easier to face something you can see than it is something that you imagine. Maybe once you write them down and face them, they will not seem as overwhelming as you first thought. No matter what you are anxious about, it will subside over time, and you can move forward. Stress can play a toll on you mentally and physically. Remember to take care of yourself.

Life, in general, will always throw us things that make us anxious, that worries us. Take steps now, as you would in your everyday life, to face them and conquer them. Be strong. Be brave. Become the new You and tackle them head-on.

LONELINESS

Loneliness often comes with being alone, and yes, it overtook me for a while and still sneaks in occasionally. The first time I felt it was after all the family left following the memorial service weekend when I was alone in the house. I found it difficult to fall asleep at night. It was too quiet. Once asleep, I would wake up in the middle of the night. After a few deep breaths and I was able to get back to sleep. I felt the loneliness more during the darkening of the evenings when I could not see outside to watch the world pass. Living in the country with few neighbors, little traffic, and no commotion to distract me, the quiet seems more pronounced.

There are times when things happen during the day, and I still want to come home and talk about it and my day. Then I remember he is not home to listen. There are times I look to where he always sat on the sofa while we enjoyed a quiet evening, both of us on our computers – together. I am learning to be my own best company. I even talk to myself more than I used to. So far, I have not lost an argument, so that is encouraging.

You will feel lonely even if your relationship was not the best. You will miss your other half. You will miss the conversations. You will miss the arguments. You will miss their touch. You will miss the shared times you had. The places you went together. You will feel lonely a lot. Learn to find that new person within yourself. One that you would consider your best friend.

Learn to do things to keep yourself busy and not feel the loneliness. Learn a new hobby. Join a group that has the same interests as you. Become more involved with your community or your church. Find something to help you overcome most of that loneliness.

I caution you about running to alcohol or drugs in an attempt to drown the feelings. Reach out to people to help you through this. Do not jump into a new romantic relationship for the sole reason to avoid being alone. You need to find You. You need to love yourself. Then, if you find someone new to share your life with, it will be wonderful and special. If you start a relationship with someone before you have accepted your loved one's death, you could end up with a failed relationship, and you may feel even worse. Each widow is different. As I and others have stated, there are no rules.

SADNESS

Being sad after someone dies is normal. I still have sad moments during this first year. I am sad that my husband is not here taking me out to dinner or going on a short road trip. Sad that he is missing out on so much of life that continues to go on even without him. Sad that I look over, and he is not sitting at the other end of the couch. So many things can cause a feeling of sadness. Sadness is different from loneliness. Sadness does not last long each time I feel it. It is mere moments when I miss him. Sometimes it is accompanied by tears. It is often a momentary emotion of wishing he was here with me to share something with, take control again, be in charge, and give me a break from being so strong. It is funny, I get sad when I have to wheel the trash can to the road for them to pick up. That was *his job*. Also sad that it takes me three to four weeks to fill that same trash can enough to put it out there for pick up. The trash can used to get full each week.

My moments of sadness come when I remember certain things. He used to tell me all the things he wanted to do in his last days before he died. He knew the meal he wanted to eat. He wanted to grab my butt one last time. He wanted to breathe one last time in my ear as he occasionally did as a private memory between us. He never got the chance. His last meal was at the hospital and was a few spoons of vanilla pudding. At least it was not green jello – he HATED Jello, especially green Jello. It makes me sad that he missed out on the things he hoped he would have had time to do in his last days.

Sadness comes in waves. You may feel fine and even be smiling one day, and the next day you are sad. You withdraw from those around you. You do not stand tall. You do not smile. Others can see the sadness in your eyes, even when you put a smile on your face and pretend you are fine. It can hit at any time. It can last a few moments or much longer.

When this feeling of sadness becomes an ongoing emotion that you cannot seem to get rid of for even a little while, you may be experiencing mild to severe depression. Before your sadness turns into depression, find someone to talk with about it. Open up about it to a friend, someone who has been through it, a therapist, or a grief counselor, someone to help you out of those deeply depressing stages. Do your best to stay strong. Do not turn to the bottle of alcohol in an attempt to drink your way out of the funk you feel. It will only take you further down the hole, and it will be harder to find daylight again. Stay strong. Understand that feeling sad is normal. You may occasionally feel some sadness for the rest of your life as you miss your loved one, the things you used to do together, and the dreams you both had. Over time the moments of sadness will be shorter and less often. The feelings may also come at the least expected moment. All could be going well, and suddenly you look up or have a thought, and immediately you feel sad from a memory or inability to share something.

WORRY

Worry. Yes, we all worry. Many things cause us to worry. I used to worry about what I would do if my husband died before me. What would I do? How would I financially survive? For many years he was unable to get life insurance. I worried a lot during those years. He finally got some, and that eased my mind a little. I worried as he purchased things with credit cards. Even opening new credit cards that had a lower interest without paying off the other ones he said he was replacing. I worried while he was in surgery. I worried a lot after he coded and then was non-responsive after they revived him. I worried. I also prayed.

My faith has always been strong. I knew God would take care of me. I knew I had at least some family and friends there for me and who would continue to be there. God certainly took care of me through all of it. It took continuously giving it all up to Him and trusting Him. There were many days of "Letting Go and Letting God." A lot of taking deep breaths and telling myself I was okay and going to get through this.

I think it is our nature to try to do everything on our own. We worry about the future. Sometimes that *future* is the next day. Our worry can include many concerns. How am I going to put food on the table? How am I going to pay all those bills? What if I have to move? *What if*? There is that awful phrase again. We begin by wondering if we had changed one thing, would our lives be different now. We continue with 'what ifing' about the future. What if I have to....? What if I can't – fill in the blank? What if no one is there for me to— fill in the blank? STOP.

Thinking that way is not getting you anywhere. Sit down. Sit back. Take a deep breath. Get some paper and a pen. Write out your concerns, and not with 'what if.' Make a list of things you need to address. Paying the bills, buying food, paying the rent or the mortgage, needing a newer car, needing a better job, etc. Now, along the other side of your list write how you are going to handle each concern. You may need to call the credit card companies about lower interest or an easier way to pay down the total, maybe even get them canceled out because they are only in your partner's name. You may want to talk to your landlord about the rent. You may need to call your mortgage company about your situation and inquire if they will work with you. There may be a lot of items on your list. There should be an equal number of solutions. If you don't know how to handle your concerns on your own, include the name of someone who may help you. That person could be a family member, a financial advisor, a Realtor, an attorney, or a mechanic, depending on what you need. Most of all – pray. Lift all your concerns, worries, fears, and your praises to Him. Then, as I occasionally put on my Facebook posts - "Let Go, Let God." Now get some much-needed rest.

ISOLATION

    I have no problem being on my own. I have always enjoyed being alone, even though I occasionally feel lonely. That feeling does not last long, nor do I dwell on it. I also know better than to isolate myself from the world. The world would miss me. Well, I hope at least some people would miss me. My part-time job gets me out of the house a couple of times a week, the same with my shopping trips for groceries or gardening supplies. Remember, I do not like to shop and avoid it as much as possible.
    I watch my grandson one day or a portion of a day each week. I have my daughter and her family over one night a week for dinner, or they have me over to their home. Although it did take me a little while before I could bring myself to go out to eat, I do go with a girlfriend every once

in a while. I have taken day trips with female friends. I even went shopping at an antique store with a male friend I had known for many years. It felt awkward, almost to the point of being wrong. It was not wrong. I was simply not ready to go with even a male close friend. I do my best not to hide in my house and avoid the public. I realize hiding in my house would not be healthy, and it certainly would not be what my husband would want me to do.

I am an introvert at heart, although I can be outgoing when I need to be. Other times – leave me alone. My husband was the more talkative one in our relationship, both in public and even when we were home. We were also both comfortable being alone and on our own.

You may think you want to stay hidden. You may think you cannot handle being out and about without your other half by your side. You may not be ready to deal with people who are still looking at you, asking how you are, and feeling sorry for you. You may fear that if you go out at all, you will do is cry. Go out anyway. Take a walk if that is all you can do in the beginning. Go people-watching. If you cannot seem to be social around other people like you used to be, at least stay in touch with a few family or friends. Then gradually find your way out. Be brave. Amaze yourself at all you can do.

Some of you are more social than others and were always out with other people and other couples. Now you find all that has changed. Couples often do not know how to treat widows. And as widows, we often feel like the odd person out in a group of couples. So we stay home. We become isolated even though we still desire to be around others. This may be the time to seek other widows who are also ready to socialize and move forward.

ENVY

This one I never imagined I would feel. Why would I envy anyone? Then I experienced it a month into being a widow. I had returned to work and saw more people. I watched couples, young and old, shopping together. I watched some holding hands. I watched some kiss. I saw their smiles and laughter. I listened to them share a conversation. I watched them walk side by side. I also saw some couples with a distance between them. I envied those that were close to each other. I wanted to run up to the ones who were distant and tell them to cherish the moments they had together and to get closer together. I refrained from approaching them as it was not my place to interfere in their lives.

I was jealous of the love and friendships I saw. We never know what we have until it is too late. It is impossible for those who have loved and now grieve to tell others how it will feel. No one understands until they are in the same situation. Through that envy, I learned to keep smiling and appreciate the love and life I had shared with my soulmate. While there were some things I regretted overall, I am so grateful for the relationship we had. I learned not to envy others and what they had. I now find myself smiling when I see couples kiss while shopping. I am happy for them. I wish I could tell them to cherish what they have and live each day to the fullest in life and love. I wish there were a way to make them understand what they have and to cherish it more. I hope most couples cherish what they have.

You may feel envious of those same things. It is hard to accept at first. You may isolate yourself because you do not want to see couples having a good time. You think it would be better to hide in the corner of your home and feel sorry for yourself. No. Instead, please do your best to take that emotion and turn it around to be happy for them. Be happy that they have this time together. Look back at your own relationship and the great times you had as a couple. Cherish those memories. Realize that at some point, you were the couple another grieving person envied. Know that we all deal with it. You may be physically on your own. You are not alone in your feelings. And, by the way, you are not alone.

FEAR

Fear. This new life I had been handed held many things I could fear. I faced the realization that I am no longer his wife. I am no longer the quiet one who stood by his side while he does all the talking (yes, that was me, quiet while he did 99% of all the talking. Funny side note here. After his memorial service, during which I read his eulogy, I talked to some of our friends, and I had one lady come up to me and tell me she had never heard me talk so much! What she said was true. Whenever we had been around her, my husband did most of the talking while I would nod my head or correct something he said.

I am no longer the quiet one. I am now the only one. I have to do all the talking. I'm an introvert! I AM quiet! I still dread having to talk on the phone. I really dread having to talk on the phone with a business when I have to argue my case. That was always something I had him do. He did it so well. I knew there was a lot I would have to change in my life because I could not let fear hold me back. In some respects, I am still holding back on my life because of my fear. One is my fear of getting lost, so I do not travel much. I plan to change that. Fear of the unknown covers a lot. There are many fears I have to face – one step at a time, one deep breath at a time.

Your fears may be similar to mine. They may be completely different. You may fear the nighttime and the quiet of your home. You may fear driving. You may fear going anywhere on your own. You may fear car trouble. You may have a fear of not knowing what to do if something goes wrong in your home or while you are out. You may fear for your safety.

For some of those fears, be proactive. Make a list of who to call if something goes wrong in your home, car, or while you are out. Write out an emergency contact list and put one in your wallet, one in your glove compartment in your car, and one in a place at your home that is easy to find. Have a person or persons listed in your phone as ICE – In Case of Emergency. So someone will know who to call for you. Take precautions at home. Install an alarm system, security lights, security cameras. Adopt a big dog. Invest in a life alert. Be sure your doors and windows are locked. Do not tell others, especially on social media, when you will not be home nor where you are going. Tell only those you trust. Hopefully, you have good neighbors that you can trust, and they will keep an eye on you. I am blessed to have such neighbors.

Do not let fear hold you back. Smile and carry on with your life. Find the new, stronger, braver you. Show the world you can carry on.

HOPELESSNESS

I think the only time I felt hopeless was a couple of weeks after my husband died. I found the floor had buckled in my basement. I was momentarily (a few hours) a mess. That was the first time I think I had a full array of emotions simultaneously – hopelessness, fear, anger, betrayal, denial, frustration. And tears! Oh, my. I was ready to give it all up at that point. I dried my tears, called the insurance company then realized it was Saturday and the local office was not open. I then racked my brain for the company we had used once when we had a pipe break and needed to dry out our basement. I finally found them. I called to have someone come dry it out. Then I called my daughter – in tears. She came over to help me move things and for moral support. I also wanted her there to help in my decision-making because, at that point, I did not trust my own judgment. It took two full days and later an argument with the company because the cost was so outrageous, but the problem was solved, and I became stronger in the end. Oh, the company won my argument over the bill.

Ten months into my journey, I needed my heat pump checked. I Googled who to call, called them, and a few hours later a technician was there. No tears, no fears. I did it!

You may feel hopeless over many things. Especially if you relied on your other half to take care of most things in your relationship. Finances. Auto repairs. Travel Arrangements. Home repair or remodel. Landscaping and mowing. Cooking, laundry, cleaning, and shopping. There can be a lot that we depend on our other half to do. Surprisingly, we do not realize how much our spouse does for us or how much we do for them until we are left with doing it all. Do not let fear or the feeling of hopelessness overtake you and keep you from learning to do everything. Even if by *doing,* you are finding people or companies to help do things for you or to teach you how to do things. We are never too old to learn.

WORKING THROUGH IT ALL

I continue to work through my grief and all the stages. I have set goals for when I want things done. Unfortunately for me, this is 2020, and our world has been hit by the Coronavirus, COVID-19 Pandemic, which slowed my time frame of reaching my goals. I had to make some adjustments to when I wanted certain things accomplished. All of my goals will eventually be reached. I was able to go through his clothes, belongings, and everything he owned and donated a lot of it. I had one yard sale and now have to put the next one on hold for a while.

I am finding the new me and liking who I am becoming. I still think I am a bit lazy some days because I do nothing except breathe and rest. I also understand that I need those days.

You will also work your way through to the other side. You will find your strength to do the things you need to do. You will find that you can breathe again, and you can live your life. You will find joy again. You will find laughter. Occasionally you will still grieve. You may revisit some of the stages and emotions of grief you thought you were passed. But as time goes on, it will be easier to handle them and move forward. They won't last as long as they did the first time you experienced them. You will be strong again. Maybe even better. You will discover who you are and love that person.

ACCEPTANCE

Yes, acceptance. That emotion I felt when I could walk into the house and accept that he would not be here. The acceptance of knowing that he was not on a trip and would call me later, or text or, better yet, be back home. The acceptance that I had to handle all the household chores and tasks on my own or find someone who could help me because he was not there to do it. The days I knew he was not going to surprise me at work. He would not call because his truck broke down, and he needed me to come to get him. The nights when I went to bed and accepted that it was me, the pillow, the sheets, and the blankets. The holidays when I knew there would be no card, no flowers, no candy, no gifts from him. The celebrations that I now attend without him. I have accepted that it is only me. A new me. A person I am learning to love more than I ever have before. I am not searching for someone who makes me happy. I am enjoying my new life. I have hope. I have faith. I have the strength to get through the rest of my life without him by my side.

You will get here as well. Have faith. Find your strength. Find your hope. Find the new You. When you do, you will be surprised. You will surprise others. Your other half will be proud of you.

Now, don't think that even when you reach this stage, your life will be perfect and free of the stages of grief. You may still feel them occasionally. You will miss your mate on the holidays, celebrations, and other special occasions. You will miss him when you find that your car won't start. You will miss him when the drain clogs up. You will miss him when you have their favorite meal. You will miss the debates and arguments, his opposing viewpoint. You will miss the things about him that used to irritate you.

THEN – one day, you will lay down in your bed ready to fall asleep and realize that you got through that day without longing for him as much. You were able to eat that meal and smile instead of tear up. You were able to get through that week, then that month, without an emotional breakdown. You will never forget. You will never totally stop grieving. You will be able to smile and pat yourself on the back for making it forward. Be proud of those times. Be proud of each step along the way. You are doing great.

All of these emotions will enter the lives of those who have lost their spouse. It helps to understand them. Prepare yourself ahead of time. I will discuss in a future chapter some things every couple can do to prepare for this time. (Further detailed in the next book I am working on.) We get so accustomed to doing things together. Each partner has a specialty they handle in their marriage. When we are suddenly handed the responsibility to do it all alone, it can be overwhelming. Take a deep breath when you are faced with this. There are people and companies out there to help you. Reach out to them. One of the hardest things to do is reach out and ask for help.

A few final words about all the emotions you go through in dealing with the stages of grief. Throughout your life, after this loss, you will be met with a sudden release of tears. It will not matter where you are, what you are doing, or who you are with at that time. The tears will come. Sometimes it will be just the urge to cry, and you will control it. Sometimes there is no stopping the tears. A song can trigger them. A certain place. A memory. A photo. Something someone says. These can each bring tears. Even after that same thing had finally brought you smiles instead, do not be concerned about the tears that flow. They are healthy. They are normal. You are doing okay. You are releasing your love, your sadness, your loneliness, your feelings for the person who was your life, your soulmate, your being, that special person. Let the tears flow. Then dry your eyes, whisper or shout your love to them, and smile. Take a deep breath. Again. Thank whoever brought those tears because that incident reminds you of your love for that person. Be glad, be happy, smile, and know that you will see your love again one day.

Chapter Two

What To Do Following Their Death

When your spouse dies there is a lot to be taken care of, and you will not feel like doing any of it. I imagine by the time you are reading this book you have taken care of most, if not all of these. For those reading this book that have not lost a loved one or that know of someone who has just lost a loved, one I hope this prepares you for this time of loss. I also hope you are not alone in taking care of all these things.

I was blessed with a family that helped me through some of this. The hospital medical staff helped prepare me for some of what I was to face. I had time before his death to talk to the organ donation agency. I had time to inquire about funeral home services and prices and make an educated decision. The staff at the funeral home I chose was very helpful and kind. I had time to prepare some things. I know many of you did not or will not have this time. However, when you do face this, know that others are there to help guide you through it all. Have someone with you to help you make wise decisions and to assure you are not taken advantage of by anyone. Sadly, some funeral homes or other companies will try to sell you more than you need or more than you want.

Over the years that my husband and I were together, we did discuss some of his final wishes. That was helpful in the decisions I had to make. I would have liked to have had them in writing so I would not have had to think so much and make final decisions independently. In my case, my husband did not have a will. I have talked with several people who had lost their spouse, and they told me they wished their spouse had had a will. They told me that without a will, things were taking years to get settled. You would think it would make things more complicated because there was no will.

In most cases, that is true. When there are young children involved, a large estate, a large family, stepfamily, or if you want specific people to have specific things. When you have certain possessions that you do Not want someone to have, for whatever reason, it is also good to have a will if you are not married but are partners or significant others. For those times when things do not automatically go to the surviving spouse, having a will is best. Each state may vary in how an estate is handled without a will. Find out what they are in your state. If there is a will, contact your attorney to address the specifics. I have heard some horror stories of family feuds and widows losing everything. I was blessed. For me, things went easy and quick. As his wife, everything automatically went to me. And I was blessed that no one in the family protested any decision I made.

To help you in your time of shock, confusion, disbelief, and utter sadness, I have written out a list of things to handle after his death. This is beneficial for when anyone has died. Feel free to add the things you need to handle, as I may not have thought of them all. I have included more details about each to hopefully answer any questions you may have. I have done my best to write them in the order of importance and the time to address them. There are some listed that may not pertain to your situation or that you choose not to do. Each of us is different with different circumstances, beliefs, and procedures regarding death and funerals.

List of Items to Handle

1. The legal pronouncement of death.
2. Arrangement of organ donation if applicable.
3. Notify family and close friends.
4. Arrange for transportation of your loved one's body.
5. Arrange care for children or pets.
6. Secure the home where they lived if they lived alone.
7. Notify their employer.
8. Look into Veteran's Benefits.
9. Decide on funeral plans, discuss with them financial arrangements.
10. Set the date for the funeral or memorial service, including time and schedule.
11. Choose funeral participants.
12. Write an obituary.
13. Order printed materials for the funeral service
14. Notification of death and funeral in newspapers and online
15. Order original and copies of the death certificate
16. Order a casket or urn and any other keepsakes
17. Order a headstone
18. Coordinate food and drinks for family and those who may spend time at the house.
19. Write a eulogy.
20. Forward their mail if they lived alone.
21. Housekeeping.
22. Create a memorial website or Facebook.
23. Start the probate process with the will, if there is one.
24. Contact the Social Security Office.
25. Notify any banks or mortgage companies.
26. Notify other financial advisors, brokers, or investment companies.
27. Contact a tax accountant.
28. Notify life insurance companies.

29. Cancel or change insurance policies.
30. Find out about any employment benefits.
31. Find and pay important bills.
32. Close credit card accounts that were in the deceased person's name only.
33. Notify credit reporting agencies.
34. Cancel the person's driver's license.

<u>*CAUTION – Reading the following may be emotional.*</u>

<u>*I am blunt in some of the detailed explanations of the above-listed items.*</u>

1. The legal pronouncement of death. This document is filled out by the doctor or hospice nurse that pronounces the death. It includes the time of death, cause of death, and place of death. This form is then used to prepare the official death certificate. If the death occurred at home ask the doctor, hospice nurse, coroner, local health department, or funeral home representative about it.

2. If your spouse is an organ donor and the death occurs at the hospital, they will help you take care of the arrangements. The tissues, eyes, skin, and so much more can be donated, not just the large organs. Also, understand that the heart may not always be able to be donated.

3. Notifying the family and friends can be divided between several people, so you don't have to do it all on your own. Most family members and friends will ask you if there is someone you would like them to contact for you. Let them help you. Have someone make a list of who has been notified, so you do your best to let everyone know who needs to know before the obituary is in the paper or on the funeral home website. Don't be surprised if you are still telling some people months later because you had no way to contact them, or somehow they got missed. They won't take it personally.

4. At the time of death, if it occurs in the hospital, they will notify the funeral home that you have made arrangements so they can come to pick up the body when it is time. If it happens at home with hospice care, the hospice nurse will call the funeral home. (See # 16).

5. If there are children that need to be taken care of, arrange for someone to help you take care of them. You should not have to do it all on your own during this time. If there are animals to be taken care of, make arrangements for someone to watch and care of them for you.

6. If for some reason the person lived alone, or if you will be away from home for any length of time, secure the home while it is unoccupied. It is also a good idea to have someone watch your home for you when it is left empty for the visitation and funeral. That is a good safety precaution for any time you are not home for any length of time.

7. Notify their employer - Companies may want to send flowers, make a donation, help in some way, even attend the funeral. There also may be insurance policies to handle or forms to fill out. Or just to let them know.

8. Look into any Veteran's Benefits the person may be entitled to. If the person was a Veteran, you might want the burial in a Veteran's cemetery with full honors. The funeral home will arrange for you to receive an American Flag in their honor, even if the funeral is not a military funeral.

9. You will need to make the funeral arrangements if these have not been made in advance. When you make funeral arrangements, they will ask you if you need to make financial arrangements to pay for it. They will work with you. If you are using the life insurance money to pay for the funeral, they will need that information. Hopefully, you have discussed with your loved one the details of their funeral. Some have special songs they want playing or something special read. There may be a specific minister they want to have speak at the service. You will also need to make arrangements for the burial.

10. Funeral date, time, and schedule. The funeral home can help with this. Rely on family members to help choose the best time to schedule a funeral. If you have a memorial service, this can be delayed for several days or weeks when it is best for all who want to attend.

11. You will need to decide who you want to be the pallbearers; the people to read the eulogies; other readings, special music, photos used, and videos to play during the service. You may also want to have other memorabilia at the funeral location. Some funerals are simple. Others that I have attended display several photos, mementos, and things that were special to or about the person.

12. Write an obituary. This one may be difficult to do. Have someone help you if you need to. I had a few days to think about what I wanted to include in the one I wrote. I suggest you have another family member or close friend read it to include everything you want. I have read a few that have forgotten to mention their spouse. Others have forgotten to mention one of the children. Double-check to make sure you have all the dates correct, the funeral's time and place, and all the details you want people to know. The funeral home will print it for you, put it on their website, or even send it to the paper for you; however, they will not edit it. They do not know the details of your loved one's life.

13. The funeral home can help with all the printed materials such as the announcements and the memorial cards. They can help with the flowers and accept the flowers delivered to the funeral home for the service if that is where the service will take place. You do not need to have the service at the funeral home. (I had the memorial service for my husband at a church).

14. Notification of death and funeral. Often it is the funeral home that takes care of printing the announcement and obituary on their website and in the local paper. Please note that often there is a fee to publish in the local paper.

15. Be sure to have enough copies of the death certificate. These will be needed for a lot of things over the next months and maybe years. Keep an original and a copy in a safe place even after you think you may not need one anymore.

16. While making the funeral arrangements, you will need to choose a casket if one has not already been selected for burial. If you are going with cremation, you can pick out an urn. If the ashes are to be scattered, you may opt to have the ashes put into a box with no urn. If the body is being cremated, you may want to order some keepsake that will have a few of the ashes inside. It could be a necklace, a ring, or other keepsakes. Other family members, such as children and siblings, may also want a keepsake.

Be aware of other options. I was shocked when the funeral director asked me if I wanted to watch as they prepared the body for cremation. So don't be surprised. I opted No on that choice.

17. Placing the order for the headstone is often taken care of by the funeral home. You can also do this on your own through a separate company. Inquire what the specifications are at the cemetery before you order. Some may only allow a flat stone. Some may specify size and style.

18. Someone will need to be in charge of any food and drinks if you will be having people at your home or another gathering place. Often friends, neighbors, or your church will offer to bring food. Let someone else be in charge, if possible. You have enough on your mind. I limited the food that was brought since no one else would be at the house after the memorial service. And the close family was going to eat out at a favorite local restaurant after the service.

19. Write a Eulogy. This can be a difficult one. Decide who will be reading the eulogy, who else will speak at the funeral or if it will only be you. Some funerals let anyone speak that wants to say something about the deceased. I had two people speak; myself and my son-in-law. We each wrote individual eulogies. Don't feel bad if you need someone to

write it for you. And don't feel bad if you are unable to stand up and read it. No one expects you to. Often it is the minister who reads it or a good friend.

20. If the person lived alone, arrange for their mail to be forwarded or stopped for a while. You may want to temporarily open a P.O. Box and use that instead of the home address for security reasons. It saves strangers coming to your home. It helps keep thieves away from your home while you are out making arrangements and attending services. Any time you will be away from home for an extended amount of time, it is always a good idea to at least put a hold on your mail delivery.

21. Have someone go through their home to get rid of any food that may spoil, plants that may need watering, or other home care needs the home may need.

22. Create a memorial page website or Facebook page. I know you can have someone designated to put a Facebook page into a memorial status if they do it in advance. I created a Facebook page of prayer while my husband was in the hospital and have kept that up as well as his regular Facebook page. Most people will leave the Facebook page up. I have a friend who passed several years ago, and her family has kept her page up. Every once in a while, someone will post a comment, missing her or thinking of her and her family. It's nice.

23. Contact your attorney to deal with the will.

24. Contact Social Security. The funeral home may do this for you, so you get your survivor's benefits. However, once you have the death certificate and you are old enough, or your spouse had already been collecting social security, you may be able to receive benefits. Contact them to see if and what you can collect. If you are over sixty, you may qualify to collect some income if your spouse collects Social Security. Call them to find out what documentation you will need.

25. Contact the bank(s) and the mortgage company. If there is a joint account, you will want to have that put into your name only or add someone else's name to the account to handle the finances if something should happen to you. I suggest waiting about a year to close a bank account until you are sure all the checks have cleared or to deposit checks that may still be arriving in that person's name. Get to know your banker. Contact the Mortgage company because there may have been a clause that the mortgage is paid off when one person on the account dies.

26. Notify all financial advisors and investment companies of the person's death and determine what you need to do to collect any funds you may be entitled to. Also, arrange with a financial advisor on ways to handle and invest your finances.

27. Contact a tax accountant, so you are prepared to deal with the taxes owed.

28. Notify the life insurance companies so you can collect them as soon as possible. Be sure to check with the person's place of employment as there may have been an insurance policy where you are the beneficiary.

29. Cancel or change the details on any insurance policies. Your life insurance beneficiary may need to be changed. Your vehicle insurances may need to be changed, homeowner's insurance will need the name changed and possibly upgraded.

30. Find out about any employment benefits in addition to life insurance.

31. Be sure to pay the important bills. Make arrangements to get them paid. Contact the companies if you need to make payment arrangements. Pay all the bills if you can. Keep your credit score up.

32. Credit cards will need to be closed or changed. If the card was in the deceased person's name, it might be closed and the balance erased, but you have to call them to have that done. If a card is in both names with him as the primary, be

careful as they may close that one as well. Open a card with only your name if you need to.

33. Notify the credit reporting agencies to avoid any fraud that may happen.

34. Notify the DMV that the person is deceased. They may want the license returned. Mine did not.

As you make the arrangements and go through all the steps of taking care of everything, do not feel bad when you cry at any moment. I am sure most of the people and agencies you will be dealing with have dealt with this before. They understand. Take your time with the things that you can take your time on. You do not have to get everything done in the first week or even the first month. Dealing with all of these things while you are emotionally missing your loved one is stressful. Take care of yourself. Get your rest. Remember to eat healthily. Take time out for yourself. Do not let others push you into doing things you do not want to do or into things you are not ready to do that can wait a little while to accomplish. Take someone with you while making arrangements at the funeral home. They will hear things you miss and be able to make sure you are making wise decisions.

Chapter Three

Becoming the New You

The funeral or memorial service is over. Your family and friends have all gone home. Your daily life has resumed. Whether that includes a house with or without children living at home, there comes a time that you look around and realize it is time to move forward. You realize that it is not good to go on day to day crying, grieving, feeling sorry for yourself, and having people worry about you. You need to do something. It is time to find the new you.

Some widows can put it simply: "Mourn, grieve, move forward." You may be thinking - How? How can I move forward when I have lost the love of my life? My soulmate? The person I did everything with? How can I move forward without my other half that made me whole?

I know for some widows this process will take longer than others. I understand how you may feel unable to move forward. That there is no life and no living without them. There is. You have learned that life is short. You tell others that your soulmate would have wanted you to keep living and to be happy again. Now is the time to tell yourself that and do all you can to make your loved one proud of you.

We all have different circumstances. Yet, we all share the same thing – our grief. We all have had a former life. The life we had when we were married. We were part of another person. Together we made a couple, a whole unit. To put it one way - Now it is time to take the doughnut with the hole in it and make it a filled doughnut. It is time to find your new life without the love of your life by your side. Know that he will always be in your heart. That transformation does take time and work.

I am experiencing this time in my life on my own. The children are grown and out of the house. One lives nearby, and they all stay in touch. My neighbors are wonderful and look out for me. My friends are there for me as well. My time at home when I awake and when I go to sleep is spent alone. Most of my time is spent alone.

I was able to take forward steps early in my grieving process. I started making changes to the house within days. I battled through my fears as I worried that people would think I was moving too fast. I was being me, and the things I did were my way of handling living again. I was not going to get stuck.

One of the fears I had before I became a widow was that if/when that time came would I become a hoarder, as I mentioned in Part One, chapter four. We all have heard the stories, seen the show, or may even know someone who is a hoarder. I have become the opposite. Not that I am getting rid of everything. I am getting rid of some things of mine and his and trying not to buy things unless I need them or use them as gifts.

Another fear I had was about finances. God has blessed me there as well. I am not rich by any means, and I still need to work. I budget my expenses and live within my income. I do not go overboard on anything if I can help it.

I was also afraid of becoming a hermit. As an introvert, I am more of a loner than a partier. I understand it is not good to stay isolated. Besides the fact it gets very lonely after a while, it is not healthy. I did have to deal with the Coronavirus Pandemic and many people being told to stay home. Many people became isolated. I had several months of being able to get out and about - before the Pandemic hit.

While staying home during the Coronavirus pandemic, I stayed in touch with people over the internet or phone.

Your life for a while may have seemed to stand still. Some have told me that the first year was all a blur when they look back years later and try to remember it. Usually, during that first year, you deal with all of the specifics; The legalities, family, friends, ceremonies, and strong emotions. The constant phone calls, arrangements, obligations. The feeling that you had to be in control and taking care of everyone. Mixed with the moments when you were able to steal away and be alone. And the moments or days when you felt so lost you could not function. Hopefully, most of the chaos is over sometime during that first year, and you have begun to settle down. That is when you realize there is a life to live - Your life, although you may not know how to get there.

We each deal with grief individually. Some handle it well, while others have a difficult time. Some find themselves stuck not knowing how to go on to the next day, let alone on with the rest of their lives. Some become stuck for years. Others jump feet first into moving forward and later find it was too fast. Some regret the moves they made. Others are doing well, have found happiness, success, new loves, and a new life. Most of us are somewhere in the middle of all that, with some days being easier than others.

When reality hits and you find yourself taking a deep breath and thinking, *'Now what,'* it is time to adjust your sails, turn the wheel and find that new route in your life. Now it is your time. You want and need to find the new you. You only see your old self. The person who had a loving partner in your life. The one you shared everything with. The one you made decisions with, compromised with, and who compromised with you to make your home and your lives comfortable and happy.

Some of you may find you don't enjoy anything about life anymore. Everything you have done for years has been with the person you lost. Finding the new you is not easy to do if you do not know who you are or even who you were when you were on your own before. Chances are the last time you were on your own was many years ago, and you may not want to be that person again. You could have been a teenager when you became a couple. You have experienced so much more of life. You have learned a lot. You have matured. You have enjoyed life and the things you did as a couple. Now you face them on your own. The things you used to do are *couple* things. Now you need to find new things that bring you joy and happiness -things to do on your own or with new people. First, you need to become a new person. And you need to learn to like and love that new person.

You will always have the memories of your spouse in your heart. You will always carry their love with you. You will always love them. They would want you to move forward. They would want you to be happy again. They would not want you to get lost in your grief. It is time to discover the new you.

So how do you do it? How do you find who the new you is? How much of the old self do you retain? Take one day at a time. Set a goal for that day. At first, it will be as easy as to breathe throughout the entire day. Next will be to go a day without crying. Next, you may want to be able to get out of your house. You may want to go someplace on your own, with a good friend or a family member. Do not hold yourself back from this opportunity. Think of it as a chance to make your late spouse proud of you.

Now is also a good time to make changes to your surroundings. You may not have touched anything since your spouse died. By making some changes, it will take you small steps forward. Think about things you could change. The first thing that came to mind and that I chose to change was my home decor. And that could be what you decide to change as well. Think about it. The home you shared is as it was for both of you. The wall color, the curtains, the furniture – all something you chose together. Do you still like it? Want to change it? Go for it! It may not be easy. It may take months or even years before you are ready. Move a piece of furniture. Change the direction your bed faces. Put up new curtains. One day you will look around, smile big and take a bigger step.

Instead of starting with your home, you may need a newer car. You may want to travel. You may want to move. As you read in part one, I made many changes to my home, which was just the beginning.

Think. Think back. Is there something that you always wanted to do? A hobby? A club you wanted to join? Skydiving? Mountain Climbing? Running a marathon? A career you never had time to pursue? Now is your time to do whatever you want to do.

I know some of these things you may have had on your bucket list were things you wanted to accomplish with your loved one. You can still do them. Find a friend to do them with if you want. Or take a moment to decide if you really still want to do them. Maybe it was something your loved one wanted to do, although deep down, you did not want to. Or now you do not want to do it because they are not here with you to enjoy it. Either way is fine. This realization is you becoming the new you. It is the time to find or create who you want to be.

I caution you not to make any major decisions too quickly, such as selling your home and moving unless you have to. It is up to you, in your time. I have widow friends who have moved and never looked back. Others are still in the house they shared with their loved one all their lives. Others who sold their home and moved, then within a year moved back to the area that was *home*.

Whatever you can think of to do or at least to try – go for it. It will help you move forward and find a new you. Baby steps. One at a time. Show everyone, including yourself, how amazing you can be.

I will add the words of advice I received for a long time after my husband's death – Take care of You. Remember to get your rest and to eat healthily. I will also add my advice – keep looking forward, keep taking one step at a time until you find yourself not only comfortable with the changes but thrilled with who you have become.

Some of you may think that when people talk about finding a new you, they are talking about finding a new love interest. That is not my focus, nor what I am referring to when I mention finding a new you. My focus is to learn who I am and how I can be now that I am on my own. Learn to love yourself and love the life you are creating and living. Then, if that time comes, and you find yourself looking or even surprised to be in a new relationship with another love in your life, that is wonderful.

I met a lady who was just shy of reaching her first anniversary of being a widow. At the one meeting we had in a group we tried to form (that didn't last), she commented that she was ready for a new love. Within a few months, she found him, gotten married, and is so happy in her new life. I say this to let you know that it does happen, and it is okay to want another love to spend your life with. I also caution you to be careful in the world of dating. Have your guard up and know what you want in your life. That is why I think it is important to find out who you are on your own first.

A personal note from me.

This book is about my first year as a widow. I cannot tell you what my life or what your life will be like years from now. I can only let you know that already in my life - I have moved forward. You read about my progress in part one of this book. I am happy most days, although I still have moments of sadness. I still have my moments of shedding tears. I also still have moments of shedding tears and being sad because my Mother and Father are not here with me. My father died in 1979, my mother died in 1990, and I still miss them both.

Yes, I have moved forward. I still have several steps to take to be where I want to be. I know who and what I want to be. I know what I have to do to get there. The world got in my way this year. I will keep going.

Chapter Four

Being Prepared

In a previous chapter I wrote about having a will, a living will, and letting your final wishes be known to your spouse and/or family. There is more to being prepared for that time in your life than having a will in place. There are ways to be prepared for living after their death. Here I will discuss ways to prepare each other to survive alone. I realize this may sound unnecessary. You may have never thought about it, or you may have thought that you would be fine when that time came. Then you read my book so far and realize there is a lot more to surviving than having a will in place. Take some time to read this chapter. I am sure there will be something you will gain from it. I have done my best to think of most things. Feel free to add things you think of as you read and make your own notes or lists. Some of what I include may not pertain to your life, and that is why I suggest making your own list using mine as a jumping-off point.

After I became a widow, I had talked with many people who told me they felt completely lost when their spouse died. I heard that before without fully understanding it. I had been alone before. My spouse and I had spent time away from each other during the years we were a couple. I had been away at least twice for schooling; I had taken trips alone; he had taken trips without me; he had been away for work. And we had survived without each other. We each had also lived on our own when we were not married to each other. Maybe those experiences helped me accept and deal with being on my own after he died.

However, I will admit this time was completely different. The emotions of it were raw. The pain was fierce. The grief and sorrow reached into the core of my bones. Then I picked myself up, knowing he would want me to keep living. He would tell me to be strong. He would want me to be happy again. Yes, it took a little while. It took less time for me than others. I realize this. It is not that I did not love him as deeply as others love. It is not that I did not care. I believe it was my faith, my resilience, and my determination. It was my knowledge of how to carry on with life and handling daily living.

Your life after the death of your spouse is one you face alone. Even if you have children at home, you now face all the responsibilities of parenting alone. The day-to-day routine of life is yours to handle. I understand that some of you are younger and have small children at home to raise. Some of you have chosen to move in with one of your adult children. Others have decided you can make it on your own. If you are not prepared, this time can be difficult. It is not impossible. If you feel lost, seek out a family member or friend who can help you. Ask your fellow church members or club members. Do not be afraid to ask for help. Taking care of your home, your family and yourself can be overwhelming. I discovered Google to be a big help for some things. I found companies to contact when I needed repairs done. I found videos to watch to help me do things on my own.

For those who are already on your journey of moving forward as a widow or widower, you may be dealing with what I will talk about in this chapter. You may wish someone had told you at least a few of these things. I hope that even though this chapter is written to all who may not have reached this time in your life that you may find a benefit in my ideas, suggestions, and advice.

The following few pages are some things to discuss with your spouse during your marriage or your relationship that will help your prepare. The reality may sound cold, while it is a fact that one day you or your partner will be the one left to carry on. Make the future easier for each other for when that time comes.

Set time aside to sit down and discuss these things with your partner. Not everyone is comfortable talking about this time in your life. My husband and I constantly put it off – forever. Luckily for me, I had paid attention to many things that he did, even if he did not know it. We also did many things together, so I was blessed to know how to do several things or who to call. Not everyone is as fortunate. By being prepared and knowing how to do everything or at least who to contact, you will have the confidence and strength to be on your own when that time comes. My husband used to tell me that if I were the one to die first, he would have no idea how to pay the bills or take care of the things I managed in our marriage. He would have called my daughter.

Ask each other a few simple questions: If one of you should die, does the other one know how to take care of everything on their own? Can you do all the things he does around the house for you and your family? Can he do all the things you do in and around the house and for the family? Think about it. What do you do that he has no idea how to do? What does he do that you do not know how to do? Once you realize how much there is to do and who does what, it is time to make some notes, if nothing else. Write down the responsibilities you take care of around the house and in your relationship. Write down what your partner does to contribute to the marriage and tasks around your home.

Discuss your capabilities to handle what the other person does. Not everyone can do everything on their own. We may not have the knowledge or the strength. While we are in a relationship with our spouse, we may not even have the desire to learn to do some things on our own. We do not see the need. Until suddenly, one day, we do.

Here is a sample of what to include in your discussion:

1) Taking care of the children
2) Paying the bills
3) Banking, balancing the checkbook, savings account
4) Mortgage
5) Handling the investments and retirement accounts
6) Home repair/maintenance
7) Vehicle repair/purchase/maintenance
8) Grocery shopping
9) Cooking
10) Cleaning
11) Lawn/land mowing, gardening, maintenance
12) Taking care of the pet(s), vet, health, walking, clean up.
13) Insurances – vehicle, home, life
14) Medical – Doctors, medications, and doses, specialists
15) Vacations, timeshares. Reservations
16) Websites
17) Funeral arrangements

I know there may be other things in your life that I have not even thought of, so add those you both do to your list.

If there are things that your partner does that you don't know how to do, these are the things you will need to at least have enough knowledge about so you can make it on your own. Same with the things you do that your partner may not know how to do.

Included in how to do them is the contact person related to each task. Who do you contact to help? Who is the contact person in each company or agency that you have business dealings with?

1) The kids! If you still have children living with you that are not adults, you both need to know a lot. You need to know what school they go to, their teachers, their homework, their after-school activities, their sports, their friends, their goals, their likes and dislikes. If they are preparing for college, know which ones they are applying. Know what they need to achieve to be accepted. For parents of small children know who their babysitters are. Understand that when their parent dies, they will need extra attention and may need someone to talk to even more than you do. They will feel lost or be angry. They will be grieving. While you take care of yourself, remember to take care of them as well. Get them the help they need. Listen to them. Let them know you are there for them. If your children are older and out of the house, you still need to be there for them as they are there for you. Take care of each other.

2) Paying the bills - Do you both know how to pay the bills? Are they paid in person, by check, online? Autopay? Do you both have the account numbers? Are you both on the accounts and have permission to handle them? (Here, you may want to discuss the credit cards. If a card is in only the deceased person's name, it may be closed when that person dies. Have at least one card in your name) If the bill-paying is online, do you both have the login and password for each one?

3) Banking - Which financial institutions do you do the banking? What are your account numbers? Are you both on each account, and do you both have access to them to make deposits, withdrawals? Do you have a safe deposit box? Do you both know where the key is? Do you know the people who work at the bank and who you need to contact to help you when you need their assistance?

4) Mortgage – Do you both have access to the mortgage account? Are you both on the account? If something happens to one of you, is your home and property paid off? Are the property taxes and insurance included in your mortgage payment? If the mortgage gets paid off, remember you are still responsible for paying the property taxes and home insurance. Make sure those are up to date. If the property taxes are not paid to date, you could risk losing your home. These are all things you both need to know.

5) Investments and retirement accounts – Do you both have the information on these to handle them? Are they through work? Do you know the contact person at the job so you can get the funds if and when needed? If they are not through work, do you both have access to what you will need? Do you know who to contact?

6) Home repair and maintenance – Do you both know who to call in case you need someone to do a home repair? Do you both know how to do the basics of simple home repair? Do you have friends that help out? Do you both know how to reach the people that help?

7) Vehicle repair, maintenance, and purchase -- Vehicles are always breaking down. A tire goes flat; a battery dies; a windshield gets cracked; an accident happens. A new car is needed. In general, it is the man who takes care of all of that. Us women are thrilled that we don't have to handle any of that. We have car trouble – we call our husband. In my case, my husband would call me to come to get him when his truck broke down, although he was the one who got the vehicles to the right garage. He was the one who made sure I had enough oil and when it was time to take it in to be changed. He was the one who even went out car shopping for me and simply brought the car to me or took me to test drive it after he had found one he thought I would like. I counted on him for all my vehicle needs. Even taking it to be washed! I only drove it and put gas in it, and if I could have had him put the gas in it, I would have. A few months before his surgery and his death, we had been car shopping. After his death – I went out and bought my own newer car! He had taught me what to look for, what to ask, and did his best to teach me to negotiate, or at the very least do my research so that I knew the price was a good one. He also taught me that before buying a car, to have a mechanic who was not related to the dealer check out the car. I had enough knowledge that at the time, that I had four mechanics I could have called on to help me. I was prepared. I was also prepared when my battery died on my old car and knew what to do – Call my neighbor! I did have the jumper cables. I also knew to leave the car running until I took it immediately to the garage for a new battery. Walmart was handy in my case.

8) Grocery shopping -- I know, you women who are reading this are now doing your best to give me *that*

look. Of course, you are the ones who do most of the shopping. Maybe! I was not. I hated shopping. Still hate shopping. My husband was the one who did 99% of the shopping as well as the cooking. I know I was spoiled. He was the one who found the good deals. He knew how to compare prices. He was the one who cut out all the coupons when those used to be more popular. He was the one who stocked up on items so we would have enough for months at a time for some things. He was the one who knew which item was in which aisle. Me? HA! I knew where the bread, milk, eggs, bananas, and salad were. I learned where more things were after he died. I also made a list and mostly stuck to that list for things I needed. If you are the one who does all the shopping, does your other half know how? Do they know what they will need to cook the meals? Do they know how to look for the best deals? Do they know how to choose the best for their needs? If they have medical issues and have to be careful what they eat, do they know what to look for and how to read a label?

9) Cooking – Here again, I know most of you women are making funny faces and questioning me. Does your spouse know how to cook? Do they know how to read a recipe? Do they know what ingredients go into their favorite meal or dessert? There is a world of spices out there, and those can get confusing. Teach each other how to cook and how to read a recipe. Show them how to operate the stove, oven, air fryer, toaster oven, pressure cooker, mixer, blender, waffle iron (that they may not even know you have). There is a lot to learn. I knew how to cook; it was a matter of fact that he was always better.

10) Cleaning – UGH. Not many people like to clean. We all love a clean house; it is the process of cleaning we detest. What products do you use to clean the house? Not all couples share the cleaning or laundry chores. Show your partner what, how, when, and where of cleaning. How much laundry detergent to use, setting the washer to the right setting, how hot to set the dryer. Do you hang the clothes to dry? Anyone still iron anything? Don't forget about the air filters on your home heating unit and the air and water filters in your refrigerator—all things you need to know how to do.

11) Lawn mowing and maintenance – Who does the mowing? Can you both operate the mower? Weed wacker? Leaf blower? Do you both help in the garden? Can you do it all on your own? Do you know where to buy the fertilizer, mulch, lawn feed, weed and insect killer? Do you know who to call to take care of all that for you?

12) The pets – Most couples who have pets take care of them together. One of you is usually the one who always takes the pets to the vet for grooming, shots, and medical emergencies. Do you both know who that is? Do you buy pet food at the store or online? Who do you order it from, what kind do you get, and how much do you order when you order it? Do you have pet insurance? Know who it is with and the cost and coverage. If the cost was an automatic payment, make sure you have the funds to cover the payment.

13) Insurances – Often, it is one person who handles all of the insurances for the two of you. Do you realize how many insurances there are to manage? Medical,

dental, vision, life. Vehicle insurance, homeowner's, or renter's insurance. Business insurances if you own a company, large or small. Do you both know which insurance company? Are your home, life, and vehicle insurance bundled with one company? Do you each have a life insurance policy? One or more? Is there a life insurance policy through your job? Medical insurance? Dental insurance? Vision Insurance? Medicare? Is all the insurance paperwork and policies in one place?

14) Medical – Family doctors, specialists, medications and their doses, and the reason for each medication. Dentist. Eye Doctor. Hospital. Workman's comp case, contacts, and details. (I did not know a lot of these details). So much of the medical world is protected by the HIPPA law, be sure you both have access to all the information you can.

15) Vacations, Timeshares, Reservations – If you frequently go on vacations, cruises, or belong to a timeshare, you may also deal with a company that handles your reservations. Have that information written down somewhere handy. Update the list of your travel plans as you enjoy them. Know whom to contact if you need to cancel them or later when you need to make future reservations.

16) Websites – We all have a lot of websites we visit. Some are for pleasure, some for household accounts, financial accounts, business accounts. We have logins and passwords. I know several couples who have a list of the logins and passwords so their spouse or a family member can get into them should they be unable to or for when they have died. I used to update our lists a couple of times a year. And still, in the end,

he had changed a few and not told me, so I could not get into some things I needed to. If there are some sites you want to keep secret, change how you think about them, or let another family member know what they are. Be open and honest with each other.

17) Funeral Arrangements – I know this is the last topic anyone wants to discuss. It will be so helpful when the time comes. In chapter three I wrote out the steps to take after a spouse dies, including things to deal with regarding the funeral or memorial service. Here are a few extra things to consider having prepared. Even if you are young and think death is a long way down the road, it is good to let your significant other know your wishes. Discuss organ donation. Have a funeral home picked out. Prepay for your funeral if possible. Have your burial plot picked out and paid for if possible.

Other funeral details to consider arranging in advance:

A) Cremation or burial. If your desire is to be cremated, include designating where you want your ashes scattered or if you want them saved so you can be scattered together.
B) Special songs you want to be sung or played at the funeral. If you want certain songs included during the funeral or memorial service, add that to your wishes and funeral plans.
C) A special poem or writing you want someone to read, and who you want to read it or not read it.
D) Photos to have on display or on the video that played at funerals. Music to play through the photo video.
E) Flowers or donations to a charity or other organization.

While we live our lives and everything is going well, we do not think of these things. We all think we will live forever. We think we will at least be the first to go. Even if we think that way, would it not be best to have everything in order, so your partner does not have to stress over the final details and how to live without you? Knowledge is key to so many things in life and for living itself.

What works for me is my file system. I will not tell you how to file things, except to suggest making it as easy as possible for yourself and your survivors. When the unexpected happens, and the survivor needs access to the insurance policies, credit card accounts, bank accounts, list of contacts, list of logins, and passwords, having them handy helps. Put everything in your home safe. Have a file drawer with hanging files for each topic discussed. Keep all your files updated each year. As you change passwords or add websites and companies you deal with, add them to your list of logins and passwords.

I have written this chapter with the understanding that when one person of the couple dies, the other one will be left to take care of and do everything on their own. These are also good things to know if one of you becomes incapacitated, in a coma, unable to communicate, unable to work, unable to do what they used to do. Become a team that works well together, so you can make the other person proud and know they won't have to worry about you when that time comes.

If you have already lost your spouse, you can still take time to make your personal list of how to take care of all these things, especially things that are not everyday things or things that you may forget. I have certain companies written down and what they specialize in for a time I may need them.

Life does go forward. The sun will rise; the sun will set even when you want it to stop for a while. Time keeps going. Make it a bit easier for yourself and those you love. Be prepared.

One last thing that many people realize when they lose someone they love and often share with others: Do these before it is too late –

Take the photos. Take the videos. Record the voices. Write the stories. Make the memories. Record the memories. So that your children, grandchildren, and great-grandchildren can know who you were.

Because in the end – We all become a memory. We all just become a story.

PHYLLIS DEWEY/HER TURN

A SAMPLE OF IMPORTANT CONTACTS

Contacts in your time of need:

I have included national numbers and websites for some. Feel free to make your own list or add the numbers and contacts here in the book.

Funeral Home _____
Contact Person _____
Phone # _____
Donate Life America 1-804-377-3580 / donatelife.net
Social Security Office 1-800-772-1213 www.ssa.gov
Insurance Company _____
Contact Person _____ Phone # _____
Insurance Policy # _____

_____
Florist _____
Contact Person _____
Phone # _____
Veterans Administration _____
Mortgage Company _____
Credit Cards

_____
Post Office _____
Phone Number _____
Babysitter _____
Phone _____
House Sitter _____
Phone _____
Neighbors _____
Name (s) _____
Immediate Family:
Names and Numbers : _____
_____
_____

Blank on purpose
For you to write notes and
add your important contact numbers.

Chapter Five

Unexpected Reality

    This chapter is about the harsh realities some widows face as they begin to move forward. I do not write this chapter to bring you down and feel depressed. I write it because the reality is something that widows do not expect, yet it happens to many widows. I hope and pray it does not happen to you, but I believe it happens to most of us to a certain degree.

    When a spouse passes away, the surviving widow faces many sudden realities. There are unexpected things that we may face. Life as a whole for us as widows has changed. It does not matter that we want it to stay the same—everything changes.

    Family, friends, neighbors, and even acquaintances will tell a widow that if there is anything they need, to let them know. We count on that. We feel a sense of security in knowing someone will always be there for us. To help us when things go wrong, or on the rough days when we just want someone to talk to or a shoulder to cry on. Someone to just be there and not even say a word, just be with us. We breathe a sigh of relief knowing we are not alone.

    Then reality sets in, and we find out those words... "If you need anything...." are just that. Words. The people behind those words are not there for us like they offered to be. This often adds to the feeling of loneliness and helplessness as we try to move forward. Many of us know someone will come to help us if we ask. In truth, we hate to ask. We feel others have their own lives with families and responsibilities, and they do not need to drop what they are doing to rescue us.

Even family members can turn their backs on you after your spouse dies. His side of the family suddenly does not invite you to special events. They do not call like they used to. If there are older stepchildren they may even walk away from you. The times they normally would have called to wish you a happy birthday or happy Mother's Day are nowadays of silence from them. Even our children may 'forget' those special days in our lives. You can't imagine that happening in your life with the relationship you have with all of your family, and I hope you are as blessed as I am that it did not happen that way. For many, it does.

The close friends you had as a couple will stop inviting you to join them when they go out or even stop calling you. Often this is because they do not know how to treat you. They do not want you to feel bad being the single person in their couple's world. They assume you will not be comfortable around them. At times, the couple will stop associating with you because the wife does not want her husband around you. After all, you are single now. I know that sounds absurd, but it happens.

Even your Facebook friends may treat you differently. Those that were once close and sent you private messages reacted to your posts, or always seemed to be there for you, are not as chatty. Some may even delete you from their friend's list.

His friends may no longer spend time in conversation with you. They were more his friends than yours. Their silence you may be able to understand.

The cold shoulder or avoidance from some may be hard to accept for a long time. You are going through enough in your life, and you at least hoped that someone would be there for you. Chances are you will have a few good friends who are there for you. Cherish them. Spend time with them. Stay in touch with as many as you can or want to.

You may be the one who no longer wants to be friends with certain people. The couple you spent time with in the past you only did because your husband liked them. Now you can choose to let them go out of your life. Now is the time in your life to make changes, and one of them is to choose friends and friendships that will be good for you. You do not need to keep those that cause you stress—the ones who bring drama into your life. You do not need more drama in your life. It would be best if you had positive, encouraging, understanding, and uplifting friends. You need people who are going to lift you. Those who understand what you are going through. Those who build you up to be a new person. Those who keep you going forward. Look for those people in your life, even if it is only one or two. Build from there. You have a life to live. A new you to find and to become. Choose those who will be there for you, even if you have to find new people to spend time with and get to know.

This distancing may even occur with fellow or former church members. You would think that Christians would be there for each other. They learned that they were to take care of the widows and the children. And most do. As I learned early on, some do not. Hold on to the ones who are there for you.

I know it is not easy to accept that some people may now ignore you. It is hard to deal with those who are not there for you when they said they would be. At first, you will try to ignore what is happening and try to make excuses for them. "They are busy', 'they have other family visiting,' 'they ... '. There are only so many excuses you can give them before realizing that it is time for you to move forward with your own life, seek other people, new people, and make new friends.

Remember, some people come into your life for a moment, some for a lifetime. Friendships come and go. The friends you had before may not understand what you are going through. The friends you make as you begin your grieving may not be the ones who stay by your side for the future. As you grow, your group of friends will grow and change.

Be careful about who you let into your circle of friends. Some may try to enter your world to take advantage of you. Some men may claim they want to be friends or more, while ultimately, they only want your money. There are so many scammers in our world today. Facebook, Instagram, dating sites, and other social media are full of them. Tread lightly. Be smart. Hang on to your money, your home, and your heart. Give your friendship and your heart only to those who earn it.

My husband and I had mutual friends as well as our individual friends. Occasionally we would go out to eat with other couples we knew or that one of us knew. After he died, I did not pursue *his* personal friends, nor did they pursue me. I did stay in touch with my friends and most of our mutual friends. I also made new friends. Once in a while, I will read on Facebook that friends have gone somewhere to eat or an event, and I wish they had invited me to go along. Then I put on my big girl panties again and shrug it off. They have their life, and I have mine. I have learned to start doing and going places on my own. Although, as I write this, it is the year 2020, and we have a pandemic going on with the rules to social distance, wear masks and avoid crowds. Plus, many places are closed. This limits where I go.

What do I want you to take from all of this? That your life will change. Many aspects of your life may change. Your immediate future will be a new learning experience that you will learn and adjust to as you progress. You will grow into a new person, one that you may have never known was a part of you. You will find strength, beauty, joy, happiness, and a different way of living.

PHYLLIS DEWEY/HER TURN

Chapter Six
Living After A Death

I wrote this book because when I searched for one on being a widow, I could not find one that fit my needs. I did a lot of internet searching. I read a lot of Facebook posts from those who had lost loved ones and lost their soulmates. I followed and still follow links that others post. I continue to learn and gain strength from others. I listened to several people I knew who had lost loved ones. Some had moved on quickly. Some remain lost, unable to take any steps forward.

Living after the death of your spouse is scary. Survivors are filled with mixed emotions and uncertainties of what they should do, when they should do it, and how they should do it. We face people watching us, judging us, seeing how we act. We hear people tell us that we should be 'over it' by now, or 'how can you do that so soon? We have the desire to make changes but are afraid to take those steps. Some don't know how to make any changes. Many stay stuck. Unable to move forward. Unable to continue living even when they know they need to. Some do not want to move forward because they think they will forget their past loved one by moving forward. You are not. You will always carry their memory with you. You can enjoy life because you know it is short and you want to make the best of it.

For all of us who have lost our soulmate, there is life after their death. We can choose when and how we want to live it. Often, as I have written, we need a group or a counselor to help us get through the stages of grief. We may need someone to help us with our finances—someone to help us learn to manage a house independently. We may need physical help in taking care of our homes and land. We may need to learn a lot of new things along the way. Many of us may need encouragement or a gentle push to start picking up the pieces of our lives. We know in our minds that we need to move forward and all that it entails. Our hearts may not be ready when others think we should be and do not understand our inability to take those steps. Eventually, we will all get there. Be kind to yourself. Be good to yourself. Learn to love yourself. Find out who you are or create the person you want to be.

For those who have lost their soulmate or a loved one, I hope this book has helped you realize the grief you are going through is normal. Whatever it is you are feeling. Wherever you are in your journey – you are okay. I also hope my story has helped you know that you can take one step at a time with a smile on your face and happiness in your heart. You can occasionally have a meltdown for a few moments or a few days. You are doing okay! You are doing great! I hope you can find peace and comfort. I hope you will be able to move forward and find joy, happiness, and, yes, love again. It may be in another romantic relationship. It may be the love of close friends and family. I hope and pray that God blesses you each day and sends you comfort. Cherish the love you had. The memories you will always carry with you. Be proud of your accomplishments, the goals you reach, and the new you that you find.

I hope this book has been an encouragement to those who have not suffered the loss of their soulmate or loved one. I hope part two has given you something to think about and take steps to make your future time easier. Know that there are others out there who have been there and done that when that time comes. There is always someone who will be there for you.

May God bless each of you as you take one day at a time. May you cherish each day and each person in your life. Enjoy all the moments. Enjoy the beauty, the love, the joy, and the happiness. Know that those will always be there. Make wonderful memories now to carry them with you always. Live life to the fullest you can. Savor the moments. Make the memories. Take the photos. Take the videos. Record the voices. Write the stories.

As my husband would always say in parting:
"God loves you, and so do I."

There is living after the death of a spouse. I am proof of that. I know many widows who are living happy lives.

I am doing things I would not even have done if he were still alive and well. I am a new me. I have my flower garden, a car that I wanted. I eat what I want (often too much). I watch TV and movies that I want. I keep the house cleaner and organized. I have no pets (Sorry, I like animals, I choose not to own one. We did have a German Shepherd for about four years that I re-homed to my grandson.) I am now an author, which was a dream since childhood. I stay up late, get up early. My life is me, my comings and goings. My timing.

Would I want him back alive and well? Of course! I miss him. I miss what we had. I also know that if he were still here, our lives would be as they always were... busy making more memories. I also know it is way past my time of wondering 'what if.' For me, it is now time to:

Follow Your Own Rhythm!
TGIF = Trust God In Faith.

Conclusion

There is no real 'conclusion' or ending of grieving. It does not matter how many years it has been since your loved one died. You will always have moments that bring sadness, tears, and even the brief return of one or more of the stages of grief. I saw a photo of my father the other day, and the tears trickled down my face. He died in 1979. I know I will always miss my husband. I truly did not think I was prepared for becoming a widow, but I quickly learned and realized how prepared I actually was. I knew more than I thought I did. By my ability to move forward, I knew I had to share with other widows.

My story of survival after my husband's death has been an inspiration to many. I notice people watching me continue living and making the best of each day. I stay positive while still having my moments of tears, loneliness, and longing for my life to be different. I am making my own life different as I continue to create the Me I want to be.

You can become your own You. Life and death are a part of living. And living after the death of your soulmate is possible. It can be beautiful. It can be positive. It is possible to fill it with happiness, laughter, and joy.

There are ways to prepare for the realities and even the unexpected truths of being a widow. There are ways to get through the stages and emotions of grieving and moving forward. Challenge yourself to find joy every day. Yes, it isn't easy to do in the beginning. Each new day allows you to take steps forward. The steps are one at a time, small and hesitant at first until you look back and are amazed at how far you have come in your life. You can smile knowing how proud your spouse would be of you.

My goal with writing this book was to be an inspiration and encouragement for other widows. It is my life story over the past year and a few months as I wrote it. In talking with my family and friends, they suggested I write it and include the second part to help others. By writing this book, I found new strength, new determination, new dreams, and set new goals. It gave me more reasons to wake up every morning. At times when I wanted to stop writing it, I would hear from other widows of how they were feeling down and not able to move forward. I heard from some who were still lost and offered them words of encouragement. I hope by sharing my story and these words of encouragement in this book that it will give many hope for their time of widowhood when it comes.

Take this book, write your notes along the way. Share it with others in reference or suggest they purchase it themselves to help them through their grief.

One of the groups that helped keep me going, which was a big inspiration to keep writing, is on Facebook. "Widowed women over 50---- moving forward in love and life." https://www.facebook.com/groups/406937413184777/

Other sources of help:

Griefshare groups are located in most areas.
Funeral homes may offer group meetings for those who grieve.
You may also find professional help through a private counselor, a grief counselor, or other doctors.
Reach out for help if you need it. Do not try to take this journey on your own. So many of us have been through what you are going through. Even if your situation is not like mine, chances are someone has been through what you are going through.

PHYLLIS DEWEY/HER TURN

Contact me:

email :
msphyllisd@gmail.com Subject Title "Her Turn."

Facebook: Phyllis Dewey
https://www.facebook.com/phyllis.dewey

My blog includes the page "After Goodbye," which was my 'almost' daily journal through that first year and that I continue to write in occasionally.
www.theflowingpenwritingcircle.home.blog

Look for my next book on widowhood, coming by the end of 2021 :

"Widowhood – Prepare, Survive, Thrive"
*Things no one ever taught you
about being a widow*

NOTES

These pages are blank on purpose.

Use them to write your notes, thoughts, feelings etc.

PHYLLIS DEWEY/HER TURN

PHYLLIS DEWEY/HER TURN

www.ingramcontent.com/pod-product-compliance
Lightning Source LLC
Chambersburg PA
CBHW051649040426
42446CB00009B/1054